Team Development Programme

A Training Manual

Joan Walton

Russell House Publishing

1167306.

First published in 2002 by:
Russell House Publishing Ltd.
4 St George's House
Uplyme Road
Lyme Regis
Dorset DT7 3LS

Tel: 01297-443948
Fax: 01297-442722
e-mail: help@russellhouse.co.uk
www.russellhouse.co.uk

British Library Cataloguing-in-publication Data:
A catalogue record for this book is available from the British Library.

ISBN: 1-903855-05-5

Typeset by TW Typesetting, Plymouth, Devon

Printed by Bath Press, Bath

About Russell House Publishing

RHP is a group of social work, probation, education and youth and
community work practitioners and academics working in collaboration
with a professional publishing team.
Our aim is to work closely with the field to produce innovative and
valuable materials to help managers, trainers, practitioners
and students.
We are keen to receive feedback on publications and new ideas for
future projects.

Contents

Author's Preface

After the *Team Development Programme* had been completed, and prior to its formal publication, it was implemented in over 20 teams. As a result, considerable experience was gained as to what was required to optimise its effectiveness. This was especially the case in relation to the question of who should be 'group leader', and what support they require. For example, in two local authorities, where the programme was implemented in several teams, managers negotiated a process whereby one manager lead or co-lead the programme for another team, and was an active participant within their own team development sessions. A formal and informal support network had been set up for all facilitators, with clear lines of communication being established with senior managers, who benefit from being aware of and informed about the developments taking place within a team.

Note: Before deciding to run the programme, carefully read the Introduction. Experience demonstrates that thorough planning and preparation will pay enormous dividends, and will ensure that constructive outcomes are achieved.

Should anyone wish to discuss in more detail issues related to implementing the *Team Development Programme*, the author can be contacted at:

Bordesley Institute
Bordesley Hall
Alvechurch
Birmingham
B48 7QB
Tel/Fax: 01527 65550
Email: jwalton@bordinst.co.uk
www.bordinst.co.uk

Acknowledgements

The creation of a training pack, such as the *Team Development Programme* is an evolutionary process, and this one has involved many people along the way. The first version of this was developed in the early 1990s, within a residential childcare context. Steve Kirk, training officer for Walsall Social Services Department, was initially responsible for providing the means and opportunity to create a context in which an in-house training programme for staff teams could be developed and tested. His continued commitment and support of this process was much appreciated. Many thanks are also due to Chris Payne, who, in his role at that time as Director of the *Caring in Homes Initiative*, a government funded project, provided the resources, which enabled this work to be developed in a way that would not otherwise have been possible. His active encouragement and support throughout were greatly valued.

Since then, many people in many places have both used this programme, and given useful feedback on it. It has stood the test of time, and is found to be as relevant now as it was when it was first created. A major point frequently made was that the team development process was relevant for many sectors and client groups, not just for staff working with children in residential settings. As a consequence of this, I have responded to requests to develop the pack in a way that makes it relevant for a wider range of contexts.

The NASA Moon Landing Exercise in Module 6 is an amended version of one that was given to me many years ago in handout form. I should like to acknowledge the creator of the original version, whose identity I have been unable to establish.

> Finally, since the original version of this pack was published, Jerry Norman, my professional and personal partner has died. His creative thinking, energy and integrity contributed greatly to the development of training materials, including those contained in this programme. He is much missed.

Joan Walton
September 2001

Introduction

Using the Programme

The *Team Development Programme* is a training pack consisting of ten modules. It has, over many years, been demonstrated to be an effective tool in helping staff teams recognise the issues that help and hinder team working, and to develop the appropriate awareness, knowledge and skills that will enable them to offer a consistent and coherent professional service.

However, like all powerful tools, if used inappropriately, it holds the potential for negative rather than positive effects. To avoid this a prospective group leader is strongly advised, before starting the programme, to:

1. Become well-acquainted with the nature of its contents, and feel comfortable about the principles on which it is based, and the training methods that are used.
2. Read carefully the *Guidance for Group Leaders* which follows, and be sure that they have the skills and experience required of group leaders. (Preferably, this should be checked out with those who know them well).
3. Have an experienced and sensitive 'supervisor' or 'mentor' who is able to provide ongoing support, and opportunities for discussion and problem-solving of issues that arise.
4. Ensure that line managers external to the team are aware that the programme is being undertaken, and are supportive of it.

A range of methods is used in the modules. The principles of adult learning provide the basis for the methods used, including:

- encouraging the full participation of team members
- acknowledging and building on previous experiences
- ensuring course contents is clearly relevant to daily practice

The Group Leader, whose main role is as facilitator, gives only a limited amount of formal input at the beginning of each session, is complemented by a comprehensive set of handouts, which can be collected to form a reference file. Input sequences are marked by ❛ ❜ and can be used verbatim. After that most sessions proceed by way of small group discussion and exercises, followed by feedback within the larger group. There are also exercises done both individually and in the whole team, with some, though limited, learning through role play.

It is important to provide a supportive, non-threatening atmosphere where team members are encouraged to develop openness and trust whilst still acquiring the ability to constructively confront each other when necessary.

Throughout the programme, there are several *Notes* which inform the group leader of difficult situations that may arise. Extra careful note should be taken of these.

However, in contexts where these factors have been taken into consideration, the benefits for team working, and consequently for the quality of service delivered, are considerable.

Guidance for Group Leaders

1. Skills and experience required

The role of the group leader in facilitating the *Team Development Programme* is crucial. The programme is written so that the minimum of practical preparation is necessary. Technically, the modules can be lifted 'off the shelf' and used as they stand. The main tasks would be to:

- become familiar with the content beforehand
- ensure that the necessary photocopying has been done
- provide appropriate materials, such as pens, A4 and flipchart paper.

However, the previous experience of the group leader is important. As a key element of the programme is the development of working relationships within a team, it is important that the group leader has some ability and confidence in working with the changing dynamics in a group situation. This means being able to pick up when there are issues arising both for individuals, and within the team, that need addressing. In addition, those parts of the programme which entail the sharing of personal information will require sensitive handling. Hence, it would be a requirement that the group leader be either an experienced trainer or groupworker; or at the least, a manager who is very used to, and skilled in, managing personal and relationship issues.

2. Who should lead the group?

Consider carefully who should fulfil the role of 'group leader', and whether they have the commitment and support from another person playing an alternative role in relation to the team. Thus, a manager running the programme with their own team should ensure that there is regular communication and support from an experienced person within their line management structure. Preferably, there would also be someone within their own team who is familiar with the programme, and who will support the implementation of planned changes, and the development of appropriate communication skills. Similarly, an external trainer should have a good working relationship with a team manager, who can feed back to the trainer issues arising within the group, and can facilitate the process of change within practice.

One model which works well is for two experienced managers to agree to run the programme for each other's teams. Thus, a manager actually remains a participating member of their team during the formal training, but can then support the process of change between the sessions. Co-training can also work well if two people feel they can work constructively together. An excellent manual for those wishing to develop training skills, and to explore the issues involved in, for example, co-working, is Armstrong, Britton and Pickles (1991), *Developing Training Skills: A Trainer's Guide to Experiential Learning*.

Here is a table showing the relative advantages and disadvantages of a group being led by an external consultant, a training officer, and a manager:

Consultant

Advantages	Disadvantages
More able to be objective.	Not in touch with group dynamics, i.e. may miss relationship issues that have strong effect on group dynamics.
Distanced from inter-agency politics.	Cannot easily pick up on issues that arise on day-to-day basis: reliant on negotiation or agreement with manager.
Can sometimes act as catalyst for change in a way which someone well known and familiar within the organisation may find more difficult: familiarity can breed contempt!	

Training Officer

Advantages	Disadvantages
May be known to team, and have developed good relationship with them, so that much of the initial groundwork already covered.	If pre-existing relationship does not exist, then issues are the same as for external trainer or consultant.
Familiar with agency procedures and customs: knows what resources are available.	If pre-existing relationship exists, but is not a positive one, then not a good start.

Manager

Advantages	Disadvantages
Known to staff, and should know them well: pre-existing knowledge of group dynamics and any hidden agendas that may affect process.	Staff may be confused over role differences: 'manager' or 'member of team' or 'group leader'. This would need to be discussed and resolved.
Able to pick up on issues in between sessions and extend content of sessions into day-to-day practice: this is in keeping with idea of encouraging reflective practice.	Too close to team members: may be too subjectively involved in issues arising. Difficult to take objective view.
	Manager's relationships with team members may be one of the issues that are causing difficulty. In this case, team members will be resistant to co-operating in the process when the responsibility for leading it is perceived by them as a cause of the problem.

3. Preparation prior to sessions

All sessions require flipchart paper and thick fibre-tip pens. If possible, contributions from small group exercises should be put on the wall during a feedback session, so blu-tack or drawing pins will be required. It is also useful to have A4 paper and pens or pencils readily available for participants to use as required. Where additional materials are needed, these are noted at the beginning of each exercise.

Although sessions can be run using information contained in the programme, suggestions for further reading are included at the end of most sessions for those wishing to read more extensively about a particular topic.

4. Support and supervision

It is important that any person undertaking this programme receives appropriate support. The programme demands much of the group leader in terms of ability to facilitate change and growth, whilst being sensitive to issues that arise both for the team as a whole, and for individuals within the team. Thus, having an experienced 'supervisor' or 'mentor' who is not directly involved in the running of the programme can be very advantageous.

5. Building Flexibility into the Programme

The *Team Development Programme* presents ten one-day modules. However, it is intended that group leaders are flexible in their use of the programme, and should modify it to suit the situation of specific staff teams.

(a) Length and frequency of sessions

The programme is planned to take place over a ten month period, with approximately four weeks between each module. However, there are alternative options that can be considered.

- The gap between modules can be shortened. It is desirable, though, to have at least two weeks between each module, to enable time for learning to be applied in practice, and for any action plans that have been agreed to be implemented.
- It may not be practical to have a team together for a full day; in this case, the course could take place for half a day every one or two weeks.
- It may be felt that the content of a particular module will take longer than one day to satisfactorily complete, or that an additional module needs to be inserted part way through the programme. In such a situation, the programme will clearly extend beyond the ten days.

(b) Timing of exercises

Prior to each exercise, there is a suggested time allowance. However, it needs to be emphasised that this is *provisional*. The exact length of time required for each exercise will depend to a great extent upon the stage of development of a group, and the extent to which participants wish to pursue specific issues that may arise.

Note: As this is a developmental programme which focuses very much on the needs of the staff team, it is advantageous if circumstances allow the group leader to be flexible with timings, when a particular discussion or debate is proving constructive. Of course, the facilitator has to make a judgement about whether the extended time is genuinely of benefit to the whole team, and will need to ensure that a minority in the group is not allowed to dominate, whilst others don't feel involved.

(c) Presenting modules in a different sequence

The *Team Development Programme* was developed in its present form in response to research undertaken with a number of teams in a local authority context. There is a logical progression in the content of these modules in that knowledge, awareness and skills acquired in the earlier stages are used and built upon in later modules.

However, it may be that an assessment of existing strengths and weaknesses within a team shows that they have already covered some of the areas, or that an issue or skill which comes later in the programme is in fact perceived to be a priority for a particular group. It is fully intended that the order in which modules are used can be changed if the needs of the team require it.

When planning such changes, it is important to be aware that the content of the first four modules is seen to be fundamental to the rest of the programme. It is suggested that prospective group leaders be very sure that the awareness and skills covered in these modules have been acquired by the team, if later modules are to be fully effective. For example, aiming to develop 'open and honest communication' (Module 8) is unlikely to achieve desired results if team members have not acquired the commitment and the skills that will enable them to give and receive constructive feedback (see Module 4).

(d) Inserting additional modules and 'troubleshooting'

Team development is unlikely to follow a trouble-free, smooth path in a forward direction, without any difficulties occurring. Modules within the *Team Development Programme* have a proven effectiveness in increasing participants' awareness and improving their ability to communicate assertively with each other. However, until well established, such skills can be fragile, and can be susceptible to damage! Group dynamics are always unpredictable, and many events can set back the process of development. Examples of such events include:

- A member of staff leaving or a new person starting work. This alters the staffing structure and influences the group dynamics.
- A team member appears to commit themselves to developing a consistent team approach, but in practice, persists in pursuing an individual course of action.
- A person has deep-seated personal problems that adversely affects their feelings and commitment to the job.

These and other issues can all affect the process of development. None are irredeemable. However, in order to counteract the effect of any one of these, there has to be an awareness of what is happening and why, accompanied by a response that deals with the issues raised. This again underpins the need for the group leader to be in touch with and sensitive to what is happening within the team; or, if the group leader is external to the group, to be in effective communication with someone who is closely involved, such as the team manager. So, for example, there has to be a means of ensuring that, as part of their induction, new members of staff are brought up-to-date with what has happened within the training process. Any team member 'sabotaging' agreed plans of action or behaving in a way that is not in keeping with the skills identified on the programme needs to be appropriately confronted. If personal issues are affecting an individual's professional performance then, again, this needs to be addressed with the person concerned.

Factors within the wider organisation can also affect team operation and motivation. This is often apparent when team members have experienced feelings of optimism through believing that team issues are being addressed, only to realise that pressures which originate outside the establishment seem to place limits on changes that can be achieved internally.

It is important to be aware of times when it would be unproductive to continue with the planned programme due to the negative 'baggage' that is being held within the team. At these points, it may be necessary to identify what the issues are which are impeding progress, and to adopt a problem-solving approach as a means of identifying ways of resolving these issues (see Module 8).

(e) Beyond the Programme

The process started by the *Team Development Programme* can be developed as far as any team may wish. When the formal modules are completed, it is important to implement action plans agreed in the final module, based on a re-assessment of the strengths and weaknesses of the team. Having established a regular 'training day', it may be beneficial to continue with this, either to consolidate team working, or to begin to introduce training in specific skill areas relevant to the agreed purpose and principles.

Principles Underlying the Programme

The Principles underlying the Programme are as follows:

1. **In the provision of a quality service, priority should be placed on effective teamworking if individual competence is to be used to the maximum benefit of the service user.**
   Individual competence will not lead to effective practice if it exists within a situation where team members behave, and make decisions, according to different sets of criteria and values. Skills practised within a context which disregards the need to address the issue of working constructively as a team, is as productive as putting good wine in rotten casks.
2. **Effective teamworking requires agreement on a common set of values and principles underlying professional practice, and establishing the purpose, aims and objectives of the unit within which the team operates.**
   Without agreement on these areas, team members are likely to be working to different agendas, which leads to inconsistent working practices. Service users will experience these as contradictory, and may respond with negative behaviours that reflect their confusion and uncertainty.

3. **Understanding the nature of discriminatory practice, and developing anti-discriminatory practice is seen to be of paramount importance.**

    During the Programme, there is an exploration of values underlying behaviours that create and perpetuate inequalities. Emphasis is placed on identifying and developing skills that support the empowerment of those who experience inappropriate discrimination.

4. **The Programme should enable all team members to be active participants in the learning process.**

    Research indicates that adults learn most effectively when they play an active role in the learning process, rather than be passive recipients of a predetermined set of answers. Thus, the programme uses training methods and techniques that encourage participants to build on knowledge and skills acquired through previous experiences, to be directly involved in determining their own development needs, and to have full opportunity to practise and gain feedback on new skills.

5. **Learning that takes place in formal training sessions should be translated into practice as fully and consciously as possible.**

    This is achieved through the idea of the 'action plan'. On a regular basis throughout the programme, team members are encouraged to write down what they aim to do in practice, and how they intend to achieve this. In a later module, progress is evaluated, with specific helping and hindering factors being identified and discussed.

6. **Criteria should be agreed that enable the quality of practice within the unit to be evaluated on a regular basis.**

    During the Programme, team members are given the opportunity to identify and discuss specific examples of practice that demonstrate that the agreed values and principles are being implemented in their work. A checklist can be compiled that forms the basis of ongoing evaluation. Consequently, a process of 'reflective practice' is introduced, encouraging team members to consciously think through what they are doing and why.

7. **Structures should be established within the unit that enable the processes of team development to be continued once the formal programme has ceased.**

    Staff meetings and supervision are seen to be the main forums within which these processes can take place. The programme places emphasis on identifying and acquiring the skills that are needed to make these forums effective in terms of enabling:
    - Efficient use of time.
    - Clear and honest communication.
    - Appropriate problem-solving and decision-making techniques.

Module 1: Establishing Purpose and Principles

? Aim

To clarify the purpose of the service which the team aims to provide, and to establish an agreed set of principles underlying their practice.

◎ Objectives

1. To discuss and agree the purpose of the team, including a clear description of the service being offered.
2. To generate a range of beliefs and principles held by individual members of staff concerning their work.
3. To agree a set of principles to which all members of the staff team would be prepared to commit themselves.

Structure of Module

1. Input by Group Leader: Purpose and Principles
2. Exercise 1.1: Statement of Purpose
3. Exercise 1.2: Statement of Principles

✎ Materials required

Flipchart, pens, blu-tack, A4 paper, pens and pencils.

Copies of handout:
- *Example of Statements of Purpose and Principles*.

⬛ Input by Group Leader: Purpose and Principles

Use the following text verbatim, if wished:

❝ Until people are clear about what it is they are trying to achieve, it is not possible to evaluate whether what they are doing is being effective or not! Further, it is likely that team members will have different ideas about what it is they are doing and why. Unless members of a staff team make explicit their own ideas and value system, individuals are likely to operate to different sets of principles and beliefs. This may lead to different work practices, which may in fact conflict with each other. Unless the reasons for these differences are clarified and discussed, practice within the team is unlikely to be as effective as it could be. ❞

✓ Exercise 1.1: Statement of Purpose

? Purpose   To clarify the purpose of the team.

Method   Large group brainstorm.
Small group and large group discussion.

Time   1½–2½+ hours.

Materials   Flipchart paper and pens, blu-tack.

↗ Process

1. The Group Leader should inform the staff team about the aim of the exercise. State that before identifying the purpose of the team, it is useful to consider what people actually do on a day-to-day basis.
2. Ask participants to brainstorm all activities undertaken in their day-to-day work: Group Leader to record on flipchart paper.
   Contributions will probably include a wide range of activities:
   - on the telephone
   - writing reports
   - talking to service users
   - counselling
   - groupwork
   - supervision
   - home visits
   - attending court

All contributions should be noted without comment.

After about five minutes, to generate further thinking, it may be helpful to suggest to team members that they imagine that they have a complete outsider in their midst, who knows nothing about why they are there, or for whom they provide a service. What do they feel are the significant aspects of what they do? For example what is the age range of service users? Does the service provide a residential facility, include family or community involvement, offer teaching or tutorial provision? Contributions may include more comprehensive statements of services provided:

- Long term residential care for older people requiring nursing care.
- Short term respite care for young people with learning disabilities.

Again, discussion at this stage should not be encouraged: this time it is to be used to note people's immediate ideas or thoughts, without evaluating or making comments on them.

Note to Group Leader: This exercise involves all team members in the process of thinking about what they do in their day-to-day work. Many are often surprised at actually how much they do do! However, thinking about **why** they do these things is rarely something they have done consciously and explicitly; and even if they have, it may not have been for a long time, nor with the whole staff group as a structured process. The next part of the exercise encourages the team to think about the rationale for these activities.

3. Break into small groups of 4-5 people. Each group should use the recorded words and phrases as the basis of discussion as to what they consider the main purpose of the team to be: i.e. in undertaking these activities, what is the outcome that they aim to achieve? This is the time for differences in thinking to be discussed.
4. Each group should write a minimum of one, and a maximum of five sentences, that establishes their agreed statement of purpose.
5. Each group's suggestion should be posted up on the wall. The different ideas can then be discussed in the large group, with the Group Leader playing a facilitative role in enabling the group to reach agreement as to the purpose of the team.

Note to Group Leader: Groups complete this exercise in various degrees of detail. This is less important than is the process of enabling the staff team to establish common ground. The outcome should be a clear statement of what the team sets out to achieve. An example is given at the end of the module.

✓ Exercise 1.2: Statement of Principles

? Purpose   To clarify a set of principles underlying practice within the team.

Method   Individual exercise; groups of 3-4; large group discussion.

🕐 Time   Minimum of 2 hours. This time will be greater if there is extensive discussion on return to the large group.

✎ Materials   A4 sheet of paper for each person; flipchart, paper and pens.

↗ Process

1. The Group Leader outlines what is meant by principles: i.e. fundamental beliefs underlying all aspects of practice within their work. Examples of principles that individuals may or may not accept would be:
   - 'I believe that children should be seen and not heard'.
   - 'I believe that all children have a right to feel valued, safe and secure'.
   - 'I believe that older people should be placed in a residential home as soon as they have problems looking after themselves'.
   - 'I believe that older people have the right to be fully supported in living in their own home for as long as they wish that to happen'.
2. Each person should have one A4 sheet of paper, which they divide into four equal pieces. Individually, all group members spend ten minutes identifying up to four principles or beliefs they hold concerning the work they do and write each one on a separate slip of paper. Each suggestion remains anonymous at this stage.
3. The Group Leader collects all pieces of paper and reads them out in turn.
4. The pieces of paper should then be laid out on a table which can be used as a point of reference during the next part of the exercise. Before breaking into small groups, team members can be given the opportunity to make a note of those principles about which they feel most strongly, to minimise the need to keep returning to the table.
5. The team breaks up into groups of 3–4 and is asked to generate up to five principles or beliefs that they agree on as a group. Emphasise that the aim of this exercise is to establish **common ground**; however any significant issues or disagreements arising from the discussion should be noted for future discussion.
6. The agreed principles should be written up on sheets of flipchart.
7. Everyone returns to the large group. The sheets of flipchart should be blu-tacked to the wall. The Group Leader can lead a discussion on issues arising from this exercise.
8. The team decides which of these principles should be accepted as a basis of practice. Final decision can be left for a further meeting, e.g. staff meeting, after there has been further opportunity for discussion and refinement of thinking.

9. Significant differences in thinking or key issues that arise from this exercise should be noted by the Group Leader. For example, some staff may state that the needs of young people are paramount; others may believe that the needs of young people and staff should be given equal priority; some staff believe that the concept of needs automatically includes those relevant to culture; others may feel that cultural needs should be specifically written into any set of principles.

Notes to Group Leader:

1. As the aim of this session is to establish common ground, it is not relevant to generate conflict by exploring issues of difference in too much depth at this stage. Issues can be highlighted as needing addressing, without beginning that process during this first session. Time, however can be spent in clarifying the nature of the differences, if this can be done constructively. You should then look for ways of picking up on these issues at later stages in the programme: preferably after team members have developed skills in giving and receiving critical and constructive feedback! (See Module 4).

2. This session generates much energy and enthusiasm. However, it is also tiring. It is advisable that team members are given the opportunity to review the outcome of their work fairly quickly, and to modify their initial set of principles if necessary. If this is to happen, then you have to ensure that the principles generated are typed up within a week of the session, with a copy given to each member of staff. They can then be encouraged to discuss them, possibly at a staff meeting, and finally agree the set of principles they will use as the basis of their practice. It can be suggested that these principles should be reviewed every 6–12 months, and modified or developed in the light of changing ideas and practice.

3. Establishing a comprehensive set of aims and objectives is not built in as an explicit session within the *Team Development Programme*. However, the *Statement of Purpose* identified within this session can be used as the basis of drawing these up, and the process started within the session can be developed. A similar methodology can be followed: that is, that individuals can be encouraged to generate initial thinking on paper, followed by discussion in small groups; finally, the Group Leader can facilitate feedback and discussion in the large group, aiming to achieve a negotiated agreement.

▣ Handout: Example of Statements of Purpose and Principles

Statement of Purpose

Our purpose is to provide home care services to the aged who are frail, younger people with disabilities, and others who would be unable to live in their own homes without some assistance. We also provide support to carers and people recovering from illness. Services may be short term providing aid in a crisis, or longer term, if in so doing it is possible to maximise or maintain a person's independence.

Principles

1. We believe that each person has a right to live in their own home if they so wish, and should be given the necessary support to do so.
2. We believe in listening actively to the service user, and discussing openly and honestly with them the most effective way to meet their needs.
3. We believe in the value of seeking resolution to conflict in points of view or best use of resources through prioritising and consensus decision-making.
4. We believe in defining and achieving excellence, and working to continuously improve the quality of our services.

Module 2: Understanding the Nature of Stress

? Aim

To develop an understanding of the nature of stress and to identify ways of managing it.

◎ Objectives

1. To determine what is meant by the term 'stress'.
2. To identify the symptoms and sources of stress both for ourselves and for others.
3. To create awareness of the links that exist between feelings of powerlessness and the experience of stress.
4. To examine the particular issues involved in belonging to certain social groupings, including black people, women and children.
5. To identify a range of ways of managing stress.

⬚ Structure of Module

1. Input by Group Leader: Stress
2. Exercise 2.1: Symptoms of Stress
3. Exercise 2.2: Experiences of Stress
4. Exercise 2.3: Sources of Stress
5. Exercise 2.4: Power and Powerlessness
6. Exercise 2.5: Methods of Coping with Stress
7. Exercise 2.6: Breathing and Relaxation
8. Further Reading

✎ Materials Required

Flipchart, pens, blu-tack, A4 paper, pens or pencils.

Copies of handouts:
- *Symptoms of Stress*
- *Physiology of Stress*
- *Sources of Stress (1)*
- *Sources of Stress (2)*
- *Methods of Coping with Stress*
- *Abdominal Breathing*
- *Relaxation Exercises*

Relaxation tape (optional).

◖ Input by Group Leader: Stress

Use the following text verbatim, if wished:

❢ "Stress" is a word that has become well-established in our culture: there are many books and articles that have been written about it. The aim of this session is to create a better understanding of what we mean by the term 'stress', and its relevance to work situations; also to be able to recognise the signs of either yourself or someone else being under stress, and the steps you might take to help.

Principles Underlying the Day

A major principle underlying the day is that the experience of stress is a normal part of life, and hence is **not** to be seen as a sign of weakness or inadequacy. Those refusing to acknowledge stress as normal are saying more about themselves and their lack of sensitivity and awareness than they are about the person admitting to feeling under pressure. However, this is not accepted in many work contexts, where people who claim to be over-stressed are stigmatised and not taken seriously.

The worth of the day's training is very much dependent on how much group participants are prepared to share with each other their own experiences of stress, and hence actively contribute to the process of understanding and increasing awareness.

Two other principles underlie the day:

1. It is not possible to separate what happens to the mind and to the body. If someone is feeling anxious or emotionally low, then their physical body is likely to react in some way, whether it becomes less resistant to viruses and illness, or to other ailments such as headaches and skin disorders. It has been suggested that many diseases, including cancer and multiple sclerosis, may often be stress-related. Similarly, if someone is physically not in good form, then they are more likely to feel depressed and under par. Even lack of sleep can affect mood and ability to handle difficult situations.
2. It is not possible to make a clear divide between what happens in your personal and professional life. However much you may try to keep the two distinct, what happens in one, will affect how you feel about the other. A bad day at work is likely to see you going home in a negative frame of mind, and vice versa.

Definitions of Stress

A psychological state of high anxiety.

(S. Fineman, 1985)

An unpleasant state of mind brought on by situations we find difficult to handle.

A combination of physical, mental, and emotional feelings that result from pressure, worry and anxiety. How you see the demands being made of you, and how you think you can cope, will determine how stressed you feel.

(J. Edwards, 2001)

(*http://www.wineconnections.co.uk/jenny/stress-a_definition.htm*)

A simple definition that can be used is: Stress occurs when pressure exceds your perceived ability to cope.

(S. Palmer, 1999)

(*http://www.managingstress.com/definition.htm*)

There is a link between what we find threatening, and how our body responds to what we feel. For example, one person might find the idea of a parachute jump extremely stressful and threatening, whilst another might revel in the prospect, feeling no fear or anxious reaction. Thus, what causes stress varies from person to person.

Physical Analogy

An understanding of the experience of stress can be aided by use of a physical analogy, which can be diagrammatically represented as follows:

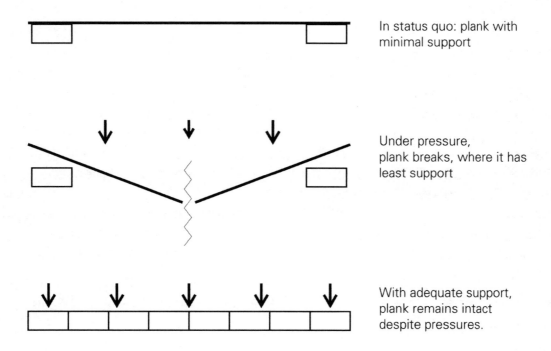

In status quo: plank with minimal support

Under pressure, plank breaks, where it has least support

With adequate support, plank remains intact despite pressures.

The individual is represented by the plank. When subject to a range of pressures, the individual, without support, will 'break'. However, given adequate support systems, a person is capable of handling a considerable degree of pressure.

Stress is Normal

Stress is a naturally occurring function. It serves a purpose: that is, it provides incentive to do things. Without a certain level of pressure to do something or go somewhere we may not have much motivation to get out of bed in the mornings! Having too little demand on you may be as damaging as having too great a demand on you. This is illustrated in the following diagram. (Draw on flipchart or whiteboard.)

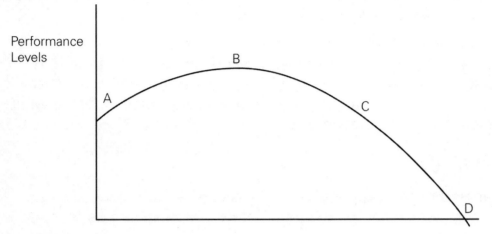

Extent of demand made on individual

A   Well able to cope, but understimulated and bored.
B   More demands made on you. You feel stretched, but able to cope: quality of performance increases.
C   Demands increase to a level that you feel is beyond you. This may be due to the fact that there is too much for you to accomplish in the available time; or you may not feel you have the required knowledge, skills or qualities. Performance starts to deteriorate, with unpleasant physical side effects being experienced.
D   Demands reach an unacceptable level. Performance deteriorates badly, leading eventually to a 'breaking point', such as physical or nervous breakdown, major illness, burnout and even attempted or successful suicide.

The aim is to find a balance where the demands made on you match your perceived capabilities. **❱**

What Happens to the Body when it is Under Stress?

See handout *The Physiology of Stress*. Go through main points.

✓ Exercise 2.1: Symptoms of Stress

? Purpose   To identify symptoms of stress.

Method   Brainstorm—record participants' suggestions on flip chart paper.

Time   15–20 minutes.

Materials   Flipchart paper and pens;
Handout: *Symptoms of Stress*.

↗ Process

1. Explain the purpose of the exercise.
2. State that one way of reducing the risk of being adversely affected by stress is to learn to recognise the very first signs of being affected by it. The symptoms of stress vary from person to person.
3. Ask participants how they know they are under stress: what signs and symptoms do they experience? Remind them of the principles of brainstorming: i.e. to state examples as they come to mind, without waiting to judge whether they are worth saying.
4. As participants call out examples, write them up on the board. If you find they are slow to respond, you can give one or two examples yourself.
5. Try to ensure you have been given examples that can fall into each of the categories of physical, psychological and behavioural symptoms. This can be encouraged by the way that you ask for examples: e.g. what do you **feel** when you are under stress; what do you **do** etc.?
6. Complete a page of flipchart paper if possible. Then ask if anyone can suggest how these examples may be categorised under three different headings: i.e. can they see a difference between different kinds of symptoms?
7. Give out handout *Symptoms of Stress*.
8. Encourage participants to add any symptoms to the list that may be relevant to themselves, but are not included.
9. Point out that the principle is 'Know Thyself'. If people can recognise quickly the signs of being under stress, they are more able to stop and identify the factors that are causing it. Then they will be in a good position to do something about it. An analogy can be drawn, of walking into a room that is pitch black. The room is full of obstacles, tables, chairs etc., and you have to negotiate a route to the other side. With the light off, you are likely to bang into objects, trip over and probably damage yourself in some way. Putting the light on, i.e. creating awareness of what is actually there, will not result in the automatic disappearance of the obstacles. However, you will be able to see them for what they are, and can look at ways of either removing the offending items, or planning a route round them that does not entail harming yourself.

✓ Exercise 2.2: Experiences of Stress

? Purpose   To encourage participants to share their own experiences of stress.

Method   Groups of 4–5.
Feedback in large group.

🕐 Time   30+ minutes.

Materials   None.

 Process

1. Tell the whole group that you are going to divide them into small groups, and that you will be asking them to share three experiences with other members of their group. At the end of the exercise they will return briefly to the large group. However, they will not be asked to share anything that was said within the small groups: that should remain confidential.
2. Tell the group that you want them to do the following:
   *Recall a situation **at work** where you have felt under stress, which you feel able to share with others in the group.*
3. Divide into small groups each having 4–5 people.
4. After 10 minutes, go round groups, and give them a second issue to discuss:
   *Recall a situation **out of work** where you have felt under stress.*
5. After a further 10 minutes, give each group the final part of the exercise:
   *Recall a situation in **either** your personal or professional life where you have been responsible for causing stress.*
6. After 30 minutes, or when all groups seem to have had the opportunity to cover all parts of the exercise, ask participants to return to the large group. Then, ask them what this exercise tells them about stress. Ensure the following points are brought out:
   - Stress is not rare: it is experienced by all people.
   - We are responsible for causing stress for others as well as being on the receiving end.
   - We are more likely to cause stress for others when we are under stress ourselves.
7. Bring the exercise to an end by pointing out that we should use this increased awareness to better understand people who are causing us pressure; it is very likely that that person, whether child or adult, is under pressure themselves. Instead of blaming them, it might be worthwhile trying to identify what might be causing the pressure, and hence increase sensitivity and understanding.

✓ Exercise 2.3: Sources of Stress

? Purpose   To identify sources of stress.

Method   Groups of 4–5.
Large group feedback.

Time   45 minutes-1 ½ hours.

Materials   Flipchart paper and pens.
Handouts: *Sources of Stress (1)*
Sources of Stress (2)

↗ Process

1. State the purpose of the exercise.
2. Give out handout *Sources of Stress (1)*. Explain that stress comes from many sources which can be categorised in a number of ways. One way of categorising it, is as identified in the handout: i.e. Personal Life; Clients or Service Users; Colleagues; Managers; Organisational Issues.
3. Give an example of what a source of stress might be under each heading: e.g. a recent bereavement would be a factor under 'personal life'.
4. Divide participants into groups of 4–5. Ask small groups to take each of the five headings identified in the handout, and to think of as many specific examples of sources of stress as they can. The aim is to provide as comprehensive a list as possible. (Ignore the heading 'Methods of Coping with Stress' for the moment). Each group should write their example on flipchart paper.
5. State time allowed (20–30 minutes).
6. Circulate round groups ensuring each is clear about the task, clarifying if necessary. Let groups know when they have five minutes left to complete the task.
7. Put completed sheets of flipchart up on wall. Suggest that the groups look at each other's list. With the large group again, lead discussion into the key issues arising from this exercise.

> Note to Group Leader: The following points can be made:
> - Many sources of stress have been identified. This can help us to understand why our work situation is experienced as stressful. In fact, given the number of issues, it would be highly surprising if any individual felt free from them at all, and hence not under any stress!
> - People at all levels of the organisation experience stress—Directors and higher managers are as likely to feel under stress as are those working at a grass roots level. The nature of the pressures may differ, but no one group should feel that any other group experience greater or lesser stress than they do.

8. Give out handout *Sources of Stress (2)*, stating that these represent examples, to which can be added those identified by themselves.

 Exercise 2.4: Power and Powerlessness

? Purpose   To explore the relationship between lack of power and the experience of stress.

Method   Groups of 4–5.
Feedback in large group.

Time   40+ minutes.

Materials   Flipchart paper and pens.

Process

1. State that you want to look at the experience of stress from an alternative perspective. You want participants to divide into three groups, each group looking at one of the following:
   - *What are the sources of stress for black people living in a white majority society?*
   - *What are the sources of stress for females living in a male dominated society?*
   - *What are the sources of stress for children living in an adult orientated society?*

   Alternatively, or in addition (depending on the size of the group), the following could be considered:

   - *What are the sources of stress for disabled people living in a predominantly able-bodied society?*
   - *What are the sources of stress for working class people living in a society where social values are largely determined by middle class people?*
   - *What are the sources of stress for older people living in a society where youth holds greater value than old age?*
   - *What are the sources of stress for homosexuals and lesbians living in a society where heterosexuality is viewed as being 'normal' behaviour?*

   > Note to Group Leader: In a mixed race group, black people should have the option of looking at issues to do with being black without being joined by white participants. In a mixed gender group, women should have the option of looking at issues to do with being female without being joined by male participants. However, no black person nor woman should feel compelled to join the groups looking at race or gender respectively, if they would prefer to consider issues to do with being a child, or any other option offered.

2. Divide into small groups for 20 minutes. Again, the main issues are to be recorded on flipchart paper.

3. Put the flipchart sheets on the wall. Bring feedback to the large group by each of the small groups in turn, followed by discussion.
4. Ensure the following points are brought out:
   - The common element shared by all groups of people being considered in this exercise is a relative experience of powerlessness: for example, black people have less power in British society than do white people.
   - There is a clear relationship between feeling powerless and experiencing stress. This results in the idea of 'oppression', where the opportunity for some people to realise their full potential is greatly limited due to the attitudes, beliefs and behaviour of others within society.
   - Consequently, although there may be a stated belief in the concept of 'equality'; equality does not in reality exist. These inequalities are due to the continuation of oppressive practices.
   - Any individual who expresses a belief in the idea of 'equality', has a responsibility to constantly seek and develop ways of recognising and eradicating oppressive practices.

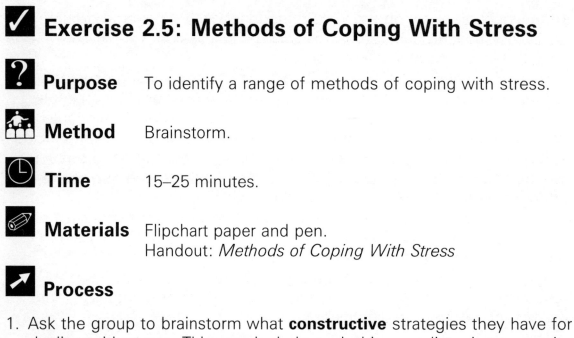

✓ Exercise 2.5: Methods of Coping With Stress

❓ Purpose   To identify a range of methods of coping with stress.

👪 Method   Brainstorm.

🕐 Time   15–25 minutes.

✏️ Materials   Flipchart paper and pen.
Handout: *Methods of Coping With Stress*

↗ Process

1. Ask the group to brainstorm what **constructive** strategies they have for dealing with stress. This may include such things as listening to music, having a bath, going for a long walk.
2. When several suggestions have been written up, point out that there may often be a fine line between positive and negative strategies. For example, having a sleep may leave you feeling more able to deal with a situation. However, if you constantly use sleep as a means of avoiding situations then it becomes a negative response. Similarly, going out for a drink with friends may be helpful; becoming an alcoholic will not.
3. After the group has generated ideas, give out handout *Methods of Coping With Stress*.
4. Emphasise that each method can be seen as one of the supporting 'bricks' identified in the initial introduction.
5. State that this session has focused on developing understanding and awareness of the nature and sources of stress; the rest of the Programme will focus on skills and techniques that can be used by individuals, and within the team, to counteract that stress.

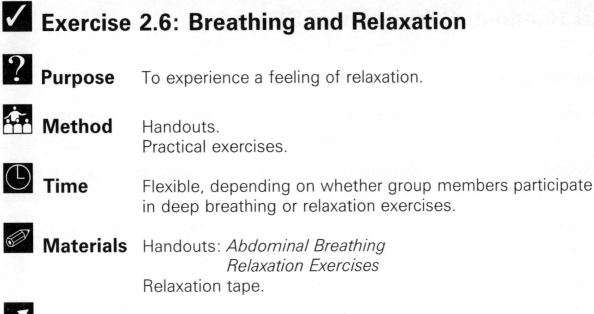

✓ Exercise 2.6: Breathing and Relaxation

Purpose   To experience a feeling of relaxation.

Method   Handouts.
Practical exercises.

Time   Flexible, depending on whether group members participate in deep breathing or relaxation exercises.

Materials   Handouts: *Abdominal Breathing*
Relaxation Exercises
Relaxation tape.

Process

1. Give out handout *Abdominal Breathing*. If wished, spend 10 minutes practising deep breathing.
2. Give out handout *Relaxation Exercises*. If wished, a relaxation tape can be played. This is an excellent means of winding down at the end of the session.

Note to Group Leader: It is helpful if this part of the session can be led by someone who is experienced in breathing techniques and deep relaxation. If the person facilitating the process is not confident and comfortable in the role, group members may well experience difficulty and embarrassment in participating fully in the activities. Should yourself or another team member have knowledge or experience of an alternative method of relaxation, then this can also be introduced into the session. Many relaxation tapes are readily available from, for example, Health Food shops.

🖭 Handout: Symptoms of Stress

Psychological	Behavioural	Physical
Tense	Over-eating	Headaches or migraines
Anxious	Over-drinking	Back pains
Worried	Not eating	Stomach disorders
Depressed	Absence from work	Hives or other skin disorders
Panicky	Insomnia	Coughs and colds
Tearful	Taking tranquillisers	Gastric ulcers
Pressurised	Short tempered	High blood pressure
Unable to relax	Unusually aggressive	Heart disease
Overwhelmed	Unusually impatient	Asthma
Loss of confidence	Switching off	Fatigue or exhaustion
Self doubt	Opting out	Muscle tension

Any others?

_____   _____   _____

_____   _____   _____

_____   _____   _____

_____   _____   _____

_____   _____   _____

_____   _____   _____

Handout: The Physiology of Stress

What is Actually Happening to the Body When it is Under Stress?

Our bodies' reaction to stress is rooted in our ancestry. In earlier times, stress had a survival value. All animals have in their make-up an emergency reaction to get themselves out of danger quickly. This is what is often called the 'Fight or Flight' or 'Alarm' reaction. When the mind perceives a threat the 'Alarm Button' or hypothalamus in the brain is pressed. The brain then sends out messages to different parts of the body, which is immediately prepared for action, system by system.

1. The muscles become tense.
2. The adrenal glands, which are situated above our kidneys, release stress hormones to get the reaction going and sustain it.
3. The heart beats faster. Blood pressure rises. The major blood vessels dilate and more blood is therefore sent to vital organs e.g. the muscles needed to run away or to fight.
4. The lungs breathe faster, which increases the oxygen supply to produce energy, and eliminate the waste carbon dioxide.
5. The liver releases glycogen (stored sugar) into the blood supply, raising blood glucose for energy.
6. Stored fats are released, again for use as energy by the muscles.
7. The skin sweats to keep us cool.
8. The pupils of the eyes dilate to improve our sideways vision to find a way of escape.
9. The digestive system slows down and almost stops temporarily, as the blood is diverted to more important organs e.g. muscles. The food stays longer in the stomach, the bowel slows down and the bowel sphincters close.
10. The bladder sphincters close.

There are many other changes, but these are the most important.

This reflex was a life-saver for our prehistoric ancestors who had to 'fight' or 'flee' regularly to save their lives. Occasionally, it is useful for us if we need to respond very rapidly on a physical level to a threat: for example, if we are charged by a bull whilst sitting in a field! A surge of energy will help us reach the gate in time.

It is an emergency reaction for use in the short term only, followed by a time for 'winding down' after the chase or the fight, during which the affected organs in the body can return to normal.

Problems develop when the reaction is sustained for longer periods of time as happens too frequently in the present day. The perceived 'threats' in modern society are less likely to be physical attacks on us. Rather, they take the form of psychological pressures resulting from the many different and often conflicting demands made on us, as we attempt to fulfil expectations of us in our various roles as workers, parents, partners, colleagues, friends etc. When experiencing 'distress' the body systems are put out of balance and then remain in this state, resulting all too often in ill health.

The irony is that what was intended as a life saving reflex is now one of the major causes of serious illness in our society.

(Adapted from *A. Brown, Remedial Massage Therapist, L.C.S.P. (Assoc)*)

Handout: Sources of Stress (1)

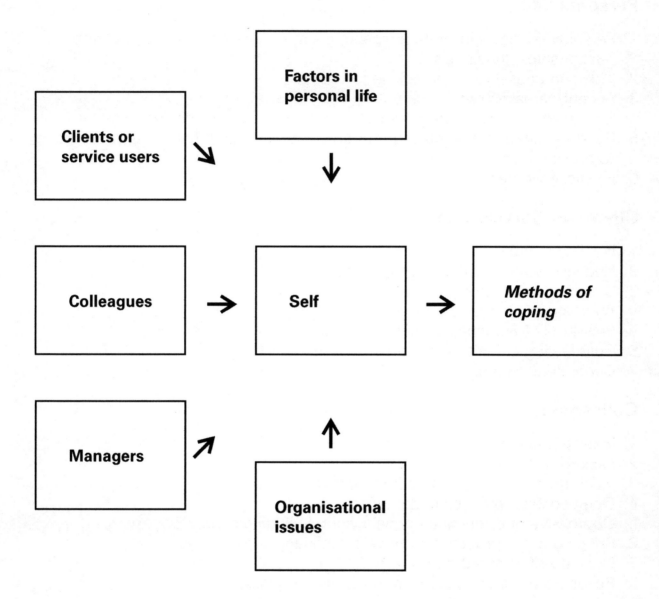

Handout: Sources of Stress (2)

Personal Life

1. Personal relationships with husband, children; 'eternal triangle'; no close relationships; loneliness.
2. Illness in oneself or in one close to oneself.
3. Recent bereavement.
4. Race-related stress: being the victim of racist attitudes or behaviour.
5. Gender-related stress: pressure to do everything; guilt (women); pressure to provide income (men).
6. Financial worries.

Clients or Service Users

1. Inability to create relationships.
2. Negative attitudes: hostility, open dislike.
3. Discriminatory attitudes and behaviour.
4. Aggressive or abusive behaviour.
5. Problems of emotional involvement; emotional pressures.
6. Guilt feelings; don't meet needs; feel responsible.
7. Dependent clients.

Colleagues

1. Inability to create relationships.
2. Lack of support.
3. 'Each doing their own thing'; no teamwork.
4. Open conflict: practice undermined.
5. Oppressive or discriminatory behaviour, including racism or sexism.
6. Bringing home problems from work: influences personality.
7. Own anxieties about work.
8. Resentful of other's positions: professional 'jealousy'.
9. Negative or pessimistic attitudes to work.

Managers

1. Lack of support: no supervision etc.
2. No attention paid to personal development.
3. 'Routines' before 'people'.
4. Little positive feedback.
5. Oppressive or discriminatory behaviour, including racism or sexism.
6. Given inappropriate work load.
7. Overworked, heavy demands.
8. Faced with crises.
9. Lack of involvement in decision making.

Organisational Issues

1. Lack of resources.
2. 'Routines' before 'people': bureaucracy.
3. Impersonal links with 'hierarchy'.
4. Poor pay or poor conditions of service.
5. 'Equal opportunities' not a reality.
6. Mismatch between professional task and administrative structure.
7. Little professional 'expertise'.
8. Administrative procedures and paperwork.
9. Lack of flexibility in determining best use of resources to meet needs.
10. Lack of clarity in roles.
11. Staffing ratios.
12. Staff shortages and vacancies not filled.

▣ Handout: Methods of Coping with Stress

1. **Diet**
   Ensure you have a balanced, nutritional diet.
2. **Sleep**
   Try to keep to a regular sleeping pattern and ensure that you sleep enough hours to enable you to wake refreshed in the morning. Most people need 7–8 hours sleep a night: making this a priority will help give you the energy to cope with other aspects of life.
3. **Organise Your Time**
   'Brainstorm' all you feel you have to do, whether it be in the short, medium or long term. Then prioritise. Determine what has to be done today and what can be postponed until tomorrow or next week. Most importantly, establish what actually does not need to be done or can be delegated to someone else. Spend 10 minutes each day reviewing this list, and bringing it up to date. Be realistic! Only plan to do what is manageable in the time at your disposal.
4. **Plan Each Day**
   Organise each day. Learn what time of day you are at your best. Ensure you eat breakfast whether or not you feel like it: this will energise your body, and help you to cope physically and mentally with the day ahead. Ensure you have regular rest periods: however pressurised take 10 minutes where you can completely cut off from your work. Go for a walk, sit somewhere on your own and relax. Eat regularly and wisely.
5. **Examine Your Lifestyle**
   Do you try too much? Imagine that you are a stranger who is looking at you from a distance. What advice would you give?
6. **Practice Mental Detachment**
   Learn to 'switch off' if you are feeling too pressurised by those around you, or if you find yourself in a boring situation which you cannot escape e.g. a traffic jam. Take yourself mentally to somewhere you would rather be. Concentrate on yourself. Consciously make efforts to relax all parts of your body and mind and think yourself into the most pleasant situation you can imagine. Do not worry what others may think: your physical and mental health is the most important.
7. **Take Positive Efforts to Improve Your Self-Image**
   You are as valuable and worthwhile a human being as anyone else! Challenge anyone who tries to put you down. Remember that those who put others down have a lot to learn themselves.
8. **Learn to be Assertive**
   That is, learn to say firmly, 'No I'm sorry, I have not the time, space, mental or physical energy to do this or take this on or cope with this'. Do not be ashamed to admit that you cannot do all that is demanded of you.

9. Relax!

Take positives moves to find means of relaxing that suits you. Sporting activities, hobbies, night classes, suit some people. Explore methods you have not tried before; yoga, deep relaxation tapes, meditation.

Do not use 'lack of time' as a reason for not choosing a specific method of relaxation: the time spent on this will more than pay dividends for other aspects of your life.

10. Seek Support From Others

Do not be afraid to ask for help, either from someone you know personally or with a professional counsellor. Sharing what you feel can in itself ease feelings of stress.

11. Alternative Medicines

Read about alternative medicines which may help deal with symptoms of stress. If you feel they may suit you, then give them a try. For example, homeopathy, Bach flower remedies, hypnotherapy.

12. Put Yourself First

If you are not OK then you are not going to be much use to others, however responsible you may feel for them. So your first responsibility is to your own welfare, and to ensuring that you are physically and mentally able to cope with your own day-to-day life. Only then will you be able effectively to help others to cope with theirs.

Making real attempts to implement some or all of the above techniques will help you to cope with stress more effectively.

▣ Handout: Abdominal Breathing

There is a close reciprocal relationship between breathing, the nervous system and the emotions. We know that fear, excitement, rage and agitation accelerate the rate of breathing which is the body's instinctive reaction to possible danger and preparation for struggle or escape. However, many of us are not aware that the process may be consciously reversed.

The nerves can be calmed and agitation or anger subdued by a deliberate slowing of the breathing rate. You can change your mental and emotional state by the way in which you breathe.

Practice this simple exercise daily. It will help you regain a calm and relaxed frame of mind and will help you to experience a few moments of stillness during a busy day. By knowing this relaxed state, you will recognise when you are moving far away from it, and be able to take some avoiding action before stress takes a hold.

In this exercise we aim to:

1. Use abdominal breathing.
2. Slow down the rate of breathing to 5-6 breaths per minute.
3. Balance the length of 'in' and 'out' breaths.
4. When this is achieved, try to make the out breath longer.
5. Relax the upper thorax.

Breathing Exercise

1. Sit or lie in a comfortable position, loosening any tight clothing.
2. Put the hands lightly on the abdomen with fingertips touching.
3. Thoroughly exhale by drawing the abdomen in so making the fingertips move together.
4. Inhale gently through the nose, allowing the diaphragm to lower and abdomen to swell, so parting the fingertips. As the inhalation continues, the lower part of the chest is expanded, so moving the ribs sideways.
5. Hold the breath in for a moment, and become aware of the expansion low down in the lungs.
6. Exhale from the base of the lungs first. The abdomen will draw in as the diaphragm lifts, and the fingertips will move together. The ribs will relax inwards as the lower lungs empty. Remain for a moment with the lungs empty before repeating the process several times until it begins to feel natural.

You will become aware of the wave like motion of the diaphragm as air is drawn in and flows out. With some practice, you will become comfortable with this abdominal breathing, and be able to practise it while walking, sitting or lying.

Aim to breathe in for the count of four heart beats, hold for two beats, breathe out for four, and remain with the lungs empty for two beats. Extend the out breath to give a 4-2-6-2 rhythm when you feel ready.

When you are first learning this exercise, it is helpful to do it with the eyes closed, and to visualise the breath flowing in and flowing out.

(From *A. Brown, Remedial Massage Therapist, L.C.S.P. (Assoc)*)

📄 Handout: Relaxation Exercises

Physical Relaxation

1. Helps to cut down fatigue, and improve recovery from fatigue.
2. Improves sleep.
3. Provides a tool to help cope with excessive anxiety and tension.
4. Aids healing and the easing of pain.

Loosening Movements

Sit on an armless chair or stool, keep your back straight and start with your head well balanced on top of your spine.

Hands:

- Let your arms hang loosely between your knees or by your sides.
- Shake your hands vigorously as though shaking off water.

Shoulders:

- Imagine that someone is lifting you by the shoulders, and that they suddenly let go. Let your shoulders drop quickly.
- Imagine you are carrying two heavy weights, and your shoulders are being pulled down. Drop the weights.
- Push your shoulders forward six times, then back six times.
- Roll your shoulders alternately, first forward six times, then backward six times.

Neck:

- Pretend your neck is broken, and allow your head to drop forward; imagining it is getting heavier. Pretend someone puts a hand under your forehead, and raises it slowly back with no effort on your part.
- Lower your head gently to the right, allowing it to sink fully under its own weight. Imagine someone lifts it gently up again for you. Repeat to the left.
- Gently turn your head from side to side, trying to look behind you, three or four times each way.

Ankles:

- Take off your shoes; cross your knees and slowly rotate each ankle in turn, six or seven times in each direction.

Thighs:

- Press your knees and thighs firmly together, then quickly release them, and allow your legs to flop apart.

(From *A. Brown, Remedial Massage Therapist, L.C.S.P. (Assoc)*)

Further Reading

Atkinson, J. (1988) *Coping with Stress at Work*. Thorsons Publishing Group.
Cooper, C. et al. (1988) *Living With Stress*. Penguin Books.
Fineman, S. (1985) *Social Work Stress and Intervention*. Gower.
Lamplugh, D. (1988) *Beating Aggression*. Weidenfield.
Powell, K. (1988) *Stress in Your Life*. Thorsons Publishers Limited.

Module 3: Developing Good Communication Skills

? Aim

To develop knowledge and skills in assertiveness as an effective means of communication; and to explore its relevance both for the learners as individuals, and as members of a staff team.

◎ Objectives

1. To understand what is meant by 'assertiveness'.
2. To be able to differentiate between assertive behaviour, and aggressive, manipulative or passive behaviour.
3. To identify situations where assertive behaviour is appropriate.
4. To consider the significance of issues related to race, gender and age.
5. To develop skills in being assertive.
6. To increase self-confidence.

◰ Structure of Module

1. Input by Group Leader: Good Communication Skills
2. Exercise 3.1: What is Assertiveness?
3. Exercise 3.2: Assertive Rights
4. Exercise 3.3: Aggressive, Passive and Assertive Behaviour
5. Input by Group Leader: Assertiveness and Self Confidence
6. Exercise 3.4: Am I Assertive?
7. Exercise 3.5: The Broken Record
8. Exercise 3.6: Becoming More Assertive
9. Further Reading

✎ Materials Required

Flipchart, pens, blu-tack, A4 paper, pens or pencils.

Copies of handouts:
- *Model of Stress*
- *Being Assertive*
- *Assertive Rights*
- *Assertive, Aggressive and Passive Behaviour*
- *Role-Play: The Double Glazing Salesman*
- *Verbal and Non-Verbal Behaviours*
- *Assertiveness and Self Confidence*
- *Assertiveness Questionnaire*
- *Developing Skills in Assertiveness*
- *Broken Record*

- *Role-plays: Broken Record*
- *A Framework for Negotiation*
- *Dealing with Conflict*
- *Setting up a Role-play*

Note to Group Leader: Handout *Model of Stress* should be distributed prior to the start of the session.

▣ Input by Group Leader: Good Communication Skills

Use this text verbatim, if wished:

❝ In Module 2, *Understanding the Nature of Stress*, the sources of stress were identified, as were a range of ways of managing it. An analogy was made with a plank, which was subject to substantial pressure, but whose resistance to breaking was directly related to the bricks that supported it. This model provides the framework for the *Team Development Programme*, and is diagrammatically represented in the handout *Model of Stress*.

One of the key methods of management is that of assertiveness, which can be identified as the basis of effective communication. The ability to be assertive is seen to be an essential skill, if the experience of stress is to be minimised, and if effective communication between members of a staff team is to be maximised. It comprises one of the main bricks that can be used to support the 'plank', and prevent it from cracking under the numerous pressures that are placed on it. ❞

✓ Exercise 3.1: What is Assertiveness?

? Purpose   To define the term 'assertiveness'.

Method   Brainstorm in large group.

Time   5–10 minutes.

Materials   Flip chart paper and pen.
Handout: *Being Assertive*

↗ Process

1. Ask the group to brainstorm what words come to mind when they think of the word 'assertiveness'. Put all suggestions on the board without comment.
2. Give out handout *Being Assertive*.
3. Ensure following points are made:
   - Assertiveness is based on the principle that all people are equal, due to their shared humanity. Thus, the idea of equality is fundamental to assertive communication; all are entitled to respect from others.
   - Consequently, all human beings have rights based on the fact that they are human, and hence no better or worse than any other human being.
   - Clearly, not all will agree as to what they want from a situation, nor what they think should happen. Hence, a further key concept in assertiveness is that of negotiation—i.e. where two or more people attempt to reach an agreement that acknowledges and respects the rights and wishes of both themselves and others.

✓ Exercise 3.2: Assertive Rights

❓ Purpose   To explore the idea of 'Assertive Rights', and to identify those rights which team members find difficult to implement in their personal or professional lives.

Method   Discussion in pairs; large group discussion.

🕐 Time   20+ minutes.

Materials   Handout: *Assertive Rights*

↗ Process

1. Pass round handout *Assertive Rights*.
2. Give the following guidelines:

   (a) Ask people to use the handout as the basis of discussion with the person sitting next to them. Suggest people take turns to read each part of the handout to each other. So, one person will read:

   > *I have the right to state my own needs and set my own priorities as a person, whatever other people expect of me because of my roles in life and you have the right to state your own needs and set your own priorities as a person whatever other people expect of you because of your roles in life.*

   The second person should then read out the second 'right'; the first person read out the third 'right'; and so on, until all rights have been read out.

   (b) As team members either read or listen to the range of rights, they should each think about what they are hearing or saying. Some of the rights they may feel they have no problem with, and generally consider that their thoughts and behaviour reflect these beliefs. However, they may find that others cause them real difficulty, either in believing them to be valid, or else, even if they believe them to be true in theory, have great difficulty in incorporating them into their day-to-day behaviour.

   (c) Partners should discuss with each other which of the rights they find difficult to accept, or live according to, and why.

   (d) Finally, each person should identify which right they find most difficult, and be prepared to feed this back to the group.

3. Team members spend 10 minutes in pairs, discussing according to the guidelines.
4. Feedback in the larger group. Ask for a volunteer to start by stating which 'right' they found most difficult, and go round the group from there. Use what people say as the basis of comment and/or discussion. For example, the following points may be raised:

(a) Numbers 1, 2, 4, 5, and 9 are found to be particularly difficult by many women, who are brought up within a society which sees women as playing a 'caring' role, and hence more inclined to put the needs of others before themselves. They are socially pressurised to look after children, partners, and other members of their families and communities, and consequently, are 'selfish' if they presume that their needs, opinions and values should receive equal attention to those of others.

(b) These same rights, and in particular number 2, also often present problems for black people. White British society adversely discriminates on the basis of colour, and has entrenched within it a belief system which views black people as inferior to white.

(c) Men can have difficulty with number 3, having been brought up in a society where males are not encouraged to share their feelings, and are pressurised to think and talk in a 'practical' way. Thus, many men have great difficulty in recognising and expressing their emotions.

(d) Number 6 states that people have the right to make mistakes, based on the belief that no-one is perfect. However, it should be pointed out that people also have to take responsibility for the mistakes they make.

(e) Many people, especially those in the helping professions, choose number 10, feeling a great sense of responsibility to find solutions to other people's problems, rather than seeing their role as enabling people to find their own solutions to problems.

(f) Most people wish to be liked by others (Number 11). However, this can result in behaviour where people are discouraged to state what they feel or need, due to a fear that others may then respond to them in a negative way. Consequently, they may give way to others; but end up feeling bad about themselves. This can cause considerable stress and anger.

5. Finish the exercise by making the following points:

(a) This version of Assertive Rights clearly represents the equality of 'you' and 'me'. Hence I am not entitled to more favourable treatment than you; neither am I entitled to less. All our interaction should be based on the awareness that we give equal consideration to each other's needs, wants and feelings.

(b) Our rights to state our own wishes often have to take into consideration our legal rights, or job rights. For example, I am entitled to get my money back from a shop if I have been given goods that were damaged when I bought them. However, if I merely decide I do not like them, I have no legal right to have my money refunded.

(c) If my boss asks me to carry out a task that I do not wish to do, but it is part of my job description, and is within my contracted working hours, then I have limited rights to refuse to carry out the task. However, if I am asked to undertake it outside my contracted hours, or it is not included in my job description, then I have the right to say 'no'. Consequently, in determining what my assertive rights are in any situation, I have to take into consideration the legal and work context.

Exercise 3.3: Aggressive, Passive and Assertive Behaviour

? Purpose To differentiate between aggressive, passive and assertive behaviour.

Method Role play in groups of five.
Feedback + discussion in large group.

Time 1–1 ½ hours.

Materials Handouts: *Assertive, Aggressive and Passive Behaviour*
Role-Play: The Double Glazing Salesman
Verbal and Non-Verbal Behaviours

↗ Process:

1. Give out handout *Assertive, Aggressive and Passive Behaviour*.
2. Read it out, or give the group time to read it to themselves.
3. State that you are going to introduce a fun exercise that will enable people to feel the difference between being assertive, aggressive and passive. This will take the form of a role play of a double-glazing salesman (noted for aggressive behaviour!), trying to sell his wares to three adjoining neighbours.
4. Give group members a copy of handout *The Double Glazing Salesman*, and go through the instructions with them, ensuring that everyone is clear about what is being asked of them.
5. Emphasise the notion of **fun**. People should not take this too seriously, and can caricature the various roles if they wish. However, the aim is to clarify the difference between different types of behaviour. The role of the observer is to take careful note of the range of verbal and non-verbal behaviours and techniques that are used to portray each role.
6. Divide the team into groups of five. Depending on the size of the team, these groups may need to be smaller or larger: however, there needs to be a minimum of four people in each group. In a group of four, omit the role of observer. In this situation, all participants should spend time after each role-play, discussing what verbal and non-verbal behaviours were used, and making a note of these. In larger groups, increase the number of observers who take notes as the role plays are carried out. Ensure everyone gets the opportunity to try out each role.
7. After role-plays are completed, return to the large group.
8. Gain feedback on how people felt carrying out the different roles. Bring out the following points:
   - Some people find some roles much harder to play than others. For example, some find it difficult to be passive, and gain feedback from others that, even when they were playing the passive role, they came across as either aggressive or assertive. Alternatively, those who are

generally passive within their existing relationships, may find it impossible to act in an aggressive way. A useful part of this exercise is finding out which behaviours come naturally, and which are enforced.

- Often, gender is seen to be a significant factor. In a society which encourages women to be submissive and caring, and men to be competitive and ambitious, women and men tend to reflect passive and aggressive behaviour respectively. However, men in residential settings playing a 'caring' role often do not fit in to the stereotypical male role. They may at times feel stigmatised as a result of this, being viewed by both men and women as 'wimps' or 'weeds'. There is tremendous pressure on men to conform to the 'macho' role in order to be seen as a 'real man'. Conversely, women who are appropriately assertive may be labelled as 'aggressive', merely because their behaviour does not fit the socially expected feminine stereotypes.

- Similarly, black people who are appropriately assertive can also be perceived as aggressive by white people operating from racist assumptions and attitudes.

- Further implications can be developed when looking at the effects of living in a society which is structured in such a way that certain groups are seen to hold more power than others. Thus, for example, children who are assertive and are able to state what they think, feel, need or want are often interpreted as 'cheeky', 'forward' or even as 'little upstarts'. The socialising of children to be submissive to the wishes of adults makes it difficult to teach them appropriate protective skills with the aim of helping deter potential abusers; and makes the aim of the abuser that much easier to achieve!

- In summary, assertiveness is the primary skill required if oppressive practices and the abuse of power are to be fundamentally challenged and eradicated. However, institutionalised attitudes and expectations in white British society make it very difficult, for those holding less power, to be assertive without being put down and labelled by others in a negative way. To be truly effective, those aiming to be assertive have to learn to deal with these responses.

9. Ask groups to feed back what verbal and non-verbal behaviour the observers noted during the role-play. Write down the range of behaviours on flipchart paper, under the three headings of 'Aggressive', 'Passive' and 'Assertive'.

10. Give out handout *Verbal and Non-Verbal Behaviour*.

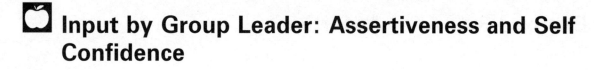 Input by Group Leader: Assertiveness and Self Confidence

Purpose   To establish the link between assertive behaviour and confidence levels.

Method   Input by Group Leader.

Time   10–15 minutes

Materials   Handout: *Assertiveness and Self Confidence*

Process

1. Give out handout *Assertiveness and Self Confidence*. Highlight link between being assertive and confidence levels. The following can be given as an example:

   You have arranged to meet a special friend for a meal at a restaurant. You are excited and looking forward to the evening, and prepare for it carefully: wash your hair, wear your best clothes, etc. When you meet your friend, it is likely that your verbal and non-verbal behaviour will reflect your mood. Your eye contact will be steady, your voice will be firm and lively, and you will radiate a positive energy.

   Imagine an alternative scenario, when you are getting ready to attend an interview for a job you very much want, but do not think you have much chance of getting. You may prepare for it in exactly the same way, paying careful attention to dress, appearance, etc. However, the person entering the interview room is likely to project a different image to the one who met the friend. Eye contact may be less steady, the voice may shake rather more, and movement may be more hesitant. In other words, your relative lack of confidence is reflected in your behaviour.

2. The aim is to use your knowledge of what is **assertive** behaviour to project a different image to that which you feel. Consequently, the technique is to act **as if** you are confident, even though you feel as though you would like the earth to swallow you up. **Feel the fear and do it anyway!** If your behaviour projects self-assurance, then others will respond to you as if you are assured. This in turn will actually help to build up your confidence levels!

3. This whole process can only be started and built on if you accept:
   - The idea of assertiveness, and the fundamental principle on which it is based: i.e. that all people are equal. Each individual is of equal value to every other individual. Anyone who oppresses another person is saying more about themselves than about the person they are oppressing.
   - People take on and fulfil different roles in life. This leads to situations where individuals hold varying degrees of responsibility, which involves some people having authority over others. However, this is no justification for one person oppressing another; the way that these roles are carried out should always convey a mutual respect between all concerned.

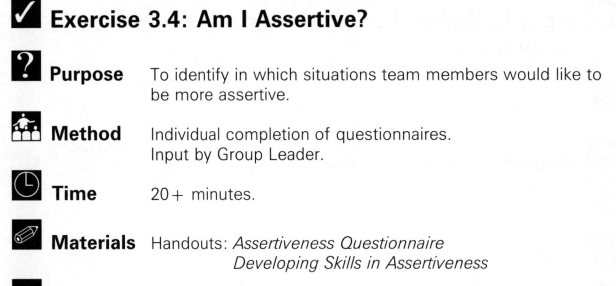

✓ Exercise 3.4: Am I Assertive?

? Purpose   To identify in which situations team members would like to be more assertive.

Method   Individual completion of questionnaires.
Input by Group Leader.

Time   20+ minutes.

Materials   Handouts: *Assertiveness Questionnaire*
Developing Skills in Assertiveness

↗ Process

1. Give out handout *Assertiveness Questionnaire*. Ask participants to complete it according to instructions, then add up the score.
2. Ask if anyone has a score of 100 or over. If so, they are already very assertive! Do not ask people to state their individual scores. State that this questionnaire is for their own consideration, to help them identify existing strengths, and to determine areas where they would like to be more assertive.
3. Highlight the fact that some people find it easier to be assertive in their personal life, and not so easy at work; for others, it is the other way round. There are two different ways of thinking that influence this:
   - In my personal life, people know me well. If I am assertive, and state what I feel and want, or challenge their ideas, they know me well enough to place my behaviour within the context of my total personality. However, people at work may not know me so well, may take my behaviour at face value, and hence are more likely to be offended, or to perceive me in a negative way.
   - I really care about the people in my personal life, and so I want to please them at all costs; however, I do not care so much what people at work think, hence I can more easily say what I feel.
4. Ask participants to identify situations in which they would like to be more assertive, in both their personal and professional lives, using handout *Developing Skills in Assertiveness* to record these on.

   Suggest they keep this list accessible, to refer to when necessary.

✔ Exercise 3.5: The Broken Record

❓ Purpose To practise the 'Broken Record' technique.

Method Input by Group Leader.
Role-play in threes.
Feedback in large group.

🕐 Time 20–30 minutes.

Materials Handouts: *Broken Record*
Role-Plays: *Broken Record*

↗ Process

1. State that a useful assertive technique is one that is often termed as the 'broken record'. This is so called because it is based on the idea that if you have a record with a scratch on it, the same few words are continuously repeated, until the listener feels so frustrated, he has to do something about it. Hence, the broken record technique is used when a person identifies a key phrase that highlights what she wishes to happen, and continues to repeat it until the listener concedes or agrees to negotiate.
2. Give out handout *Broken Record*, and give time for team members to read it, and ask questions for clarification.
3. Emphasise that in using this technique, the assertive person has to remain calm, relaxed, in control, but determined that the other person is not going to dominate or manipulate them. Reinforce that the aim is to reach a resolution that respects the rights of both parties.
4. Divide the team into groups of three. Give out copy of handout *Role-Plays: Broken Record*. State that each person takes a turn at being assertive, being on the receiving end of the assertive response, and being the observer. Ensure that all are clear about the instructions.
5. After 10–15 minutes, return to large group. Lead discussion as to what happened in each role-play. After comparing the different responses, highlight the following issues:
   - **Requesting a cup of coffee:** In this situation, the customer has a right to a hot cup of coffee. The generally accepted principle is that, when it is difficult to prove who is at fault, the customer's perspective is accepted. Consequently, if the waiter or waitress refuses to remedy the situation, the customer's next move would be to call the manager.
   - **Buying the apples:** It is important to focus on the issue, and avoid getting into a 'win-lose' situation if possible. It is possible that both customer and shopkeeper are genuine in what they want: i.e. the customer requires a pound of apples of the same quality as are on display; and the shopkeeper has other apples that are of the same quality. Thus, his move should be to offer the customer the opportunity to check the quality of the other apples. In other words, there is room for negotiation. However,

if the shopkeeper knows that the other apples are inferior, and continues to refuse to sell the ones on display, the only right that the customer has is to take her trade elsewhere: and perhaps to let others know what kind of service she received at this particular shop!

- **No-smoking sign:** This is probably the most difficult situation of the three. The non-smoker has no more rights than the smoker; and there is little scope for negotiation. It is the person who has responsibility for the waiting room who has the rights in this situation. The no-smoking sign suggests that the next move for the non-smoker, given an unresponsive smoker, is to inform the receptionist or doctor.

✓ Exercise 3.6: Becoming More Assertive

? Purpose   To further develop knowledge and skills in assertiveness.

Method   Input by Group Leader.
Role-play and discussion in small groups of 4–5 people.

🕐 Time   Including roleplay: 1½–2½ hours (depending on size of small groups).
Role-play being replaced by small group discussions of individual situations: 1–1½ hours.

✎ Materials   Handouts: *A Framework for Negotiation*
Dealing with Conflict
Setting up a Role-play

↗ Process

1. Give out handout *Framework for Negotiation*.
   Read through it with the group, giving an example of how it might apply in practice: i.e. a woman and man, sharing a home, where both are in full time work. Traditionally, the woman has done all household chores. She feels her male partner should take an equal share, and decides to raise this as an issue.
2. Give out handout *Dealing with Conflict*. State that the difference between this and negotiation is the higher levels of emotion involved.
   Go through this handout, again giving an example of how it might apply in practice: but in this situation, the woman has raised the issue on many occasions, with little or no change in her partner's behaviour. She has become increasingly frustrated and angry.
3. Point out that, before being assertive, it is important to identify:
   - What your rights are, bearing in mind constraints imposed by, for example, law or by a work contract.
   - What lengths you are prepared to go to in order to have your wishes and feelings responded to. For example, in the situation described above, the woman would have to decide whether she was prepared to leave the relationship if she was unsuccessful in negotiating a reasonable compromise; or if her emotional dependency on her partner was too strong to allow her to break away, and hence she would be forced to revert to a passive role within the relationship. In other words, if someone feels they cannot face the consequent changes that might result from being assertive, they may then make a deliberate choice not to be, and to stay in the situation that currently exists.
4. Ask each person to identify a situation in which they would like to be more assertive, and which they would be prepared to share with 3–4 others. State that they are going to have the opportunity to develop their assertive skills in the setting of a small group (no-one is expected to role-play in the large group).

5. Distribute handout *Setting up a Role-Play*. Go through it with team members, and ensure that they are clear about what they are being asked to do.
6. The team breaks up into small groups. It is important, if at all possible, that each group works in a different room, or in an uninterrupted setting.
    Every team member has 20-30 minutes to use the group to focus on their situation.
7. Initially, the Group Leader can ensure that everyone is clear and comfortable about what they are doing. Generally speaking, groups should be left to work on issues on their own. However, it may be necessary to stay with some groups to act as facilitator.
    Some may choose not to role-play, and to spend time on discussion. (This will be the case particularly if resources do not allow for separate rooms). As long as discussion is found to be of value, it should not be discouraged. However, those groups who have the 'courage' to role-play generally find the outcome more beneficial.
8. Feedback in large group. The aim of this is to identify what people learned, and to share any negative or positive feelings. No questions should be asked as to the actual content of the situations discussed; this should remain confidential to the small group, unless the person responsible for raising the situation wishes any aspects of it to be shared.

🖳 Handout: Model of Stress

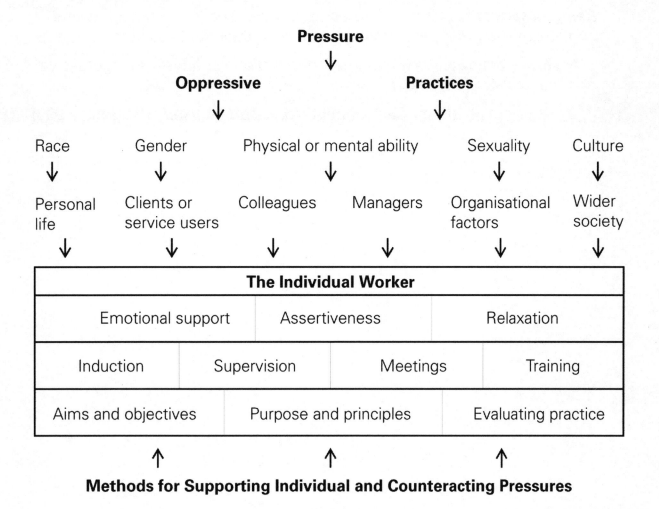

Methods for Supporting Individual and Counteracting Pressures

◳ Handout: Being Assertive

Being assertive is being able to communicate clearly our needs, wants and feelings to other people, without abusing their rights as human beings.

Assertive behaviour is an alternative to passive(submissive), aggressive and manipulative behaviour.

(From Gael Lindenfield, *Assert Yourself*, Thorsons, 1986)

▣ Handout: Assertive Rights

| '**I**' | **and** | '**You**' |

'**I**'   **and**   '**You**'

1. I have the right to state my own needs and set my own priorities as a person, whatever other people expect of me because of my roles in life.

1. You have the right to state your own needs and set your own priorities as a person, whatever other people expect of you because of your roles in life.

2. I have the right to be treated with respect as an intelligent, capable and equal human being.

2. You have the right to be treated with respect as an intelligent, capable and equal human being.

3. I have the right to express my feelings.

3. You have the right to express your feelings.

4. I have the right to express my opinions and values.

4. You have the right to express your opinions and values.

5. I have the right to say 'yes' or 'no' for myself.

5. You have the right to say 'yes' or 'no' for yourself.

6. I have the right to make mistakes.

6. You have the right to make mistakes.

7. I have the right to change my mind.

7. You have the right to change your mind.

8. I have the right to say 'I don't understand'.

8. You have the right to say 'I don't understand'.

9. I have the right to ask for what I want.

9. You have the right to ask for what you want.

10. I have the right to decide for myself whether or not I am responsible for finding a solution to another person's problem.

10. You have the right to decide for yourself whether or not you are responsible for finding a solution to another person's problem.

11. I have the right to deal with people without having to make them like or approve of me.

11. You have the right to deal with people without having to make them like or approve of you.

▣ Handout: Assertive, Aggressive and Passive Behaviour

There are three basic kinds of interpersonal behaviour: assertive behaviour, aggressive behaviour, and passive or submissive behaviour.

Assertive behaviour

Assertive behaviour involves standing up for your own rights, in any situation, and in such a way, that you do not violate the rights of other people. It involves expressing your needs, wants, views and feelings in a direct, honest and appropriate way.

Assertive behaviour is based on the belief that, in any situation:

- You have needs to be met and so do the other people involved.
- You have rights and so do other people.
- You have something to contribute, and so do other people.

Assertive behaviour does not necessarily mean getting what you want.

The aim of assertive behaviour is to work towards satisfying the needs and wants of all parties involved in a situation.

Aggressive Behaviour

Aggressive behaviour involves standing up for your own rights, in any situation, but doing so in such a way that at the same time you violate the rights of other people. It involves expressing your needs, wants, views and feelings in inappropriate ways, and ignoring, disregarding or discounting the needs, wants, views and feelings of other people.

Aggressive behaviour is based on the belief (which may not be conscious) that:

- Your own needs, wants, views and feelings are more important than those of other people.
- You have rights but other people do not.
- You have something to contribute but other people have little or nothing to contribute.

The aim (which may not be conscious) of aggressive behaviour is to 'win' if necessary at the expense of the others involved in a situation.

Passive or Submissive Behaviour

Passive behaviour involves failing to stand up for your own rights in any situation, or doing so in such a way that other people can easily disregard them or disregard you. It involves failing to express your needs, wants, views and feelings, or doing so dishonestly, apologetically or diffidently.

Passive behaviour is based on the belief (which may not be conscious) that:

- The other person's needs, wants, views and feelings are more important than your own.
- The other person has rights but you do not.
- The other person has a great deal to contribute, but you have little or nothing to contribute.

The aim (which may not be conscious) of passive behaviour is to avoid conflict and to please or placate other people.

(With acknowledgement to K. and K. Back, *Assertiveness at Work*, McGraw-Hill, 1986)

⬛ Handout: Role-play: The Double Glazing Salesman

Aims of Role-play

1. To give learners a chance to have fun and learn in a small group setting where they can relax and have a laugh!
2. To find out what verbal and non-verbal behaviours are respectively associated with aggressive, submissive/passive and assertive forms of communication.

Role-players

Double-glazing salesman
Aggressive householder
Submissive householder
Observers
Assertive householder

Scenario

1. One person is to play a double glazing salesman, who is calling at a number of adjoining houses. His aim is to sell double glazing; or at the very least, to ensure that he can persuade the householder to agree to make an appointment to have a 'free' survey undertaken, in order that the householder might receive appropriate advice on heating bills and how noise might be reduced. The salesman has received intensive training which has encouraged him to be extremely insistent about making an appointment, and not to accept 'no' as an answer. If the householder is unwilling to talk immediately about the possibility of buying double-glazing, he persists in saying that he merely wants to do a survey and give some free advice. If the householder refuses to make an appointment, the salesman asks them what reasons they have for refusing this free offer.
2. The others play adjoining neighbours: one aggressive, one submissive, and one assertive, etc. Each realises that it would be a mistake to allow the salesman into the house, and that they should not make a further appointment to see him. The neighbours should try to behave in the way described in the handout *Aggressive, Passive and Assertive Behaviour*, and appropriate to their role. (Behaviour can be caricatured or exaggerated as much as is wished).
3. Each interaction should take 2–3 minutes.
4. The role-play starts with the salesman going to a 'door', knocking, and waiting for an answer.
5. Everyone should have a turn at all roles.

Observer's Role

- Each group should have a sheet of paper, with three headings 'Aggressive', 'Submissive', 'Assertive'.
- The observer should record under the appropriate heading the verbal and non-verbal behaviour that communicates a certain form of behaviour. For example, the observer may be watching the 'aggressive' householder, who, during the role play, repeatedly points their finger, and shouts very loudly. These behaviours can be noted as being indicative of some-one being 'aggressive'. (It is important, however, to be aware of cultural differences, and to discuss these within the group when appropriate. For example, there are cross-cultural variations in interpretations of tone of voice or eye contact.)
- After the role-plays are completed, each small group will be asked to feed back the behaviours recorded by the observers to the large group.

📖 Handout: Verbal and Non-Verbal Behaviours

Aggressive Behaviour:

Verbal	**Non-Verbal**
Swearing or abusive statements Shouting or over-loud voice Threats or threatening questions Blame put on others Sarcasm and other put-downs Others? _____ _____ _____	Pointed finger Clenched or shaking fists Piercing eye contact Folded arms Forward posture Others? _____ _____ _____

Passive or Submissive Behaviour:

Verbal	**Non-Verbal**
Frequent 'ums' and 'ers' Frequent justifications Soft voice Constantly apologising (I'm sorry but . . .) Self put-downs ('I'm not the right person to decide this really') Long, rambling sentences Stammering Others? _____ _____ _____	Fidgety hands Shuffling feet Avoiding eye-contact Stoop Others? _____ _____ _____

Assertive Behaviour:

Verbal	**Non-Verbal**
Making statements that are brief, clear, and to the point Distinguishing between fact and opinion Making suggestions that are not weighted with advice Finding out the thoughts, opinions, and wants of others Suggesting ways of compromising or getting round problems Others? _____ _____ _____	Steady, direct eye contact Listening to the other person Staying calm and in control Relaxed posture Upright posture Others? _____ _____ _____

▣ Handout: **Assertiveness and Self Confidence**

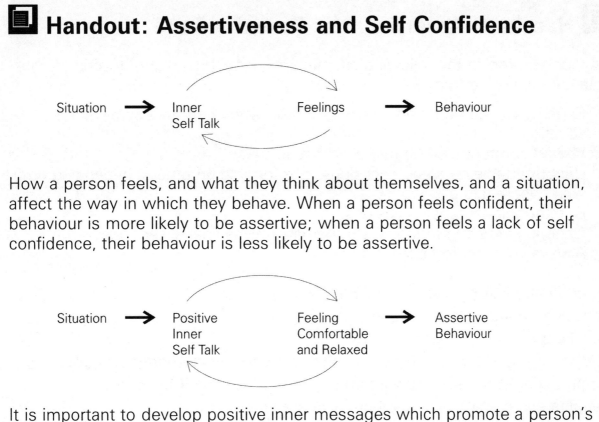

How a person feels, and what they think about themselves, and a situation, affect the way in which they behave. When a person feels confident, their behaviour is more likely to be assertive; when a person feels a lack of self confidence, their behaviour is less likely to be assertive.

It is important to develop positive inner messages which promote a person's sense of their own value and self-worth. For example, 'I have a number of valuable qualities, such as loyalty, generosity, and a sense of humour.' Positive self talk tends to lead to assertive behaviour.

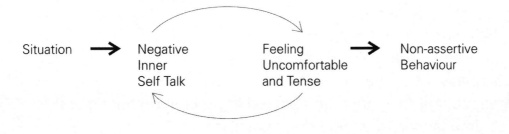

People can often be very negative about themselves and their own abilities, in a way that denies their sense of self worth. It is important for a person to challenge these thoughts and to build on positive statements.

(Adapted from Townsend A., *Assertion Training*. FPA Education Unit, 1985.)

◼ Handout: Assertiveness Questionnaire

How do you feel in the following situations? For each situation described, rate yourself on a scale from 0–5, as follows:

0   Extremely uncomfortable on any occasion when I am faced with this situation.
1   Very uncomfortable on most or all occasions
2   Uncomfortable on some occasions, comfortable on others (depending on who, where, etc.).
3   Comfortable on most occasions.
4   Generally very comfortable, with perhaps occasional exceptions.
5   Always very comfortable.

Entering and leaving a room which is full of people: _____

Speaking up and asking questions in a meeting: _____

Speaking in front of a large group: _____

Stating your ideas and opinions to someone who is in authority over you: _____

Commenting when someone interrupts you at the time it happens: _____

Keeping eye contact with someone you are speaking to: _____

Receiving a compliment about the way that you look: _____

Asking someone, without apologising, to return an item they have borrowed: _____

Asking for a service which you expect, but have not yet received (e.g. in a shop, restaurant, etc.): _____

Returning faulty goods to a shop: _____

Telling an unwanted door salesman to go away: _____

Discussing openly someone's criticism of you: _____

Telling someone that they are doing something that is bothering you: _____

Refusing to do a favour when you don't want to: _____

Expressing anger when you feel angry: _____

Challenging someone who has made a racist comment: _____

Challenging someone who has made a sexist comment: _____

Telling a friend you want an evening to yourself when they phone to invite themselves round: _____

Responding to a member of your family who asks you to do something just as you have settled down to a good book: _____

Telling someone you are late for a meeting when they are talking to you about their wonderful holiday: _____

Telling a friend that you have just put your meal out when they phone up for a chat: _____

Refusing to do overtime, or sleep in at short notice, when requested to do so by your boss: _____

Receiving praise from your boss for some work you have done: _____

Total: _____

▣ Handout: Developing Skills in Assertiveness

In order of most importance to you, make a list of up to ten situations in which you would like to become more assertive; i.e. No. 1 is the situation in which you would **most** like to become more assertive etc. These situations can be taken from any aspect of your life i.e. at work, at home, with family or friends, with 'strangers' (e.g. shopkeeper, waiter, salesman) etc.

Having done that, write down how you behave now in each of these situations (e.g. aggressively or submissively or passively). If you avoid a situation, this counts as passive behaviour. If you find that you behave differently at different times, then write down all your responses.

Should you have difficulty in thinking of situations, look at the *Assertion Questionnaire* which you completed in the previous exercise, and use your responses to this to help guide your thinking.

Situation	**Present Response**
1. _____	_____
_____	_____
2. _____	_____
_____	_____
3. _____	_____
_____	_____
4. _____	_____
_____	_____
5. _____	_____
_____	_____
6. _____	_____
_____	_____
7. _____	_____
_____	_____
8 _____	_____
_____	_____
9. _____	_____
_____	_____
10. _____	_____
_____	_____

▣ Handout: Broken Record

Broken Record is the skill of being able to repeat over and over again, in an assertive and relaxed manner, what it is you want or need, until the other person gives in or agrees to negotiate with you.

The aim is to:

- Be specific about what it is you want or feel.
- Stick to your statement, repeating it over and over again, if necessary.
- Don't get diverted by other people's responses.

This technique is useful in situations when:

- Your rights are in danger of being abused.
- You are likely to be diverted by clever, articulate but irrelevant arguments.
- You are likely to lose self-confidence, because you know you could be affected by 'put-downs' and 'digs' from the other person.

The advantage of this approach is that once you have decided what your 'key phrase' is, you can relax—because however abusive or manipulative the other person tries to be, you know exactly what you are going to say. As well as getting your message across, you will find repetition strengthens your own sense of conviction, and increases your determination.

As you gain confidence in this technique, you may be able to develop it, so that you slightly change the words that you use each time: but remember to identify and repeat your **key phrase**.

Don't let **manipulative bait**, **irrelevant logic**, or **argumentative bait** put you off.

Example:

Selma has bought some French cheese from a shop, which, when opened at home, is found to have rather more mould than it should have had. She returns it to the shop.

Selma:	I bought this cheese yesterday. When I got home and opened it, I found it was mouldy. I want my money back, please.
Shopkeeper:	Nothing to do with me, I wasn't here yesterday. (Irrelevant logic).
Selma:	I bought it in this shop and as it is inedible, I want my money back, please.
Shopkeeper:	That sort of cheese is meant to be mouldy. If you don't like that sort of thing, you shouldn't buy it. (Argumentative bait)
Selma:	I know what kind of cheese I buy. This is bad, and I want my money back.
Shopkeeper:	Look, there's a queue of people waiting behind you. Please would you let them pass. It's not fair they should have to wait. (Manipulative bait).
Selma:	I can see that there are people behind, but I bought this cheese yesterday. It is inedible, and I want my money back.
Shopkeeper:	Well, how much was it then? (In a resigned, unfriendly voice, but nevertheless, he gives the money back).

(Example taken from Anne Dickson, *A Woman in Your Own Right*.
Quartet Books, 1982).

▣ Handout: Role-Plays: Broken Record

Select one of the following situations to practice the 'broken record' technique.

- You are sitting in a cafe. The cup of coffee that has been brought to you is cold. Ask for a hot cup of coffee in replacement.
- You see some apples you want on display in the greengrocers. You ask for a pound of these—but the greengrocer goes to another box of apples, which you suspect are not as good as the ones you have seen. You are only prepared to buy the apples on display.
- Someone sits beside you in the doctor's waiting room, which has a large 'no smoking' sign on the wall, and proceeds to light up a cigarette. You want him to put it out.

Alternatively, you can select a situation within your own experience, where you think that the broken record technique could be effectively used.

▣ Handout: A Framework for Negotiation

1. Choose the right time
Part of the art of successful negotiating is knowing when it is a 'good time' to bring up a problem. It is worthwhile agreeing a time to sit down and have a joint discussion, rather than attempting to present a problem when the other person is occupied with something else.

2. Present the problem in a constructive way
If possible, plan ahead. Think about what points you want to make, and how you might put them.

3. Anticipate counter arguments
Think about arguments the other person may introduce, and work out how to respond to them.

4. Be specific
Don't go round in circles. This only has the effect of confusing, and clouding the real issue: keep to the point. Use the 'broken record' technique if necessary.

5. Be tactful
The way we approach someone is important; being sarcastic or unpleasant only results in the other person becoming defensive and resistant to change.

6. Explain how the other person's behaviour affects you
Focus on how you feel. Take responsibility for how you feel, saying e.g. 'I feel angry, because . . .' rather than 'you have made me angry . . .' Explain, rather than 'tell the person off'.

7. Listen attentively
Concentrate and attempt to understand what the other person is saying and feeling, asking for clarification if necessary. Let the person know that you have heard them.

8. Be prepared to compromise
The point to remember is that the issue is not about winning or losing, but about reaching a compromise that is acceptable to both parties. It can be helpful to offer a compromise.

9. Show willingness to find an acceptable solution
Emphasise that you are willing to explore how an outcome acceptable to both of you can best be achieved.

▣ Handout: Dealing With Conflict

The following outlines the steps you can take for assertively resolving a situation, where someone has made you angry. They are similar to steps for Negotiating, but involve a higher intensity of emotion, which has to be properly handled if effective negotiation is to take place.

1. **Acknowledge your own feelings honestly**
   Do you feel angry, humiliated, afraid, or depressed, etc?

2. **Identify the problem**
   Decide exactly what your grievance is, and what remedy you require.

3. **Prepare your case**
   Discuss your grievance and feelings with others, ensure that your case is understood, get advice, think it out from all angles, get support, rehearse expressing your case.

4. **Arrange a meeting**
   Decide where and when the encounter should take place, and who you would like present. Choose a time and place which are best for you if you can, and decide if you wish to have any allies or mediators present.

5. **State your grievance:**
   There are a number of important aspects to this:
   - **Feelings first:** When emotions are strong, deal with feelings first. Rational discussion comes later after feelings have cooled.
   - **Show respect for the other person:** Remember that even though you disagree, the other person's view of the situation is probably as honestly held as yours. Disagree with their view of the situation, but do not denigrate them as a person.
   - **State your own feelings, views and required remedy:** Be brief. Avoid loaded or abusive words. Say what you mean, and mean what you say. Disclose how you really feel.

6. **Listen to the other person's case**
   Listen carefully, until you experience the other person's position. Repeat the case back to them, so they know you've listened. Use their words for any touchy issues.

7. **Discuss differences**
   Repeat steps 5 and 6 if necessary.

8. **Reach agreement if possible**
   Possible outcomes are:
   - Your case and the remedy you require are accepted.
   - Your case and the remedy are rejected.
   - Your case and the remedy are partly accepted.
   - You agree to differ.

9. **Assess the encounter**
   Think through the encounter, and learn from it.

Handout: Setting up a Role-Play

In setting up a role-play, you can follow these stages:

1. Each person should identify a situation where they would like to be more assertive, and that they are willing to share with members of the group.

2. One person (A) volunteers their situation for the group to focus on.

3. (A) explains their situation to the rest of the group, e.g.:
   My mother insists on buying sweets for my three-year-old daughter. I have told her on many occasions that we do not want her to get used to having too many sweets, and that we would prefer her to buy something else. However, she just replies that the role of grandparents is to 'spoil' children, and a few sweets will not hurt her. I end up losing my temper, and getting nowhere!

4. Other members of the group volunteer to take on the other roles involved, e.g. in the above example, someone (B) would volunteer to be (A)'s mother.

5. (A) describes to (B) how his mother might behave in this situation in as much detail as possible, e.g.:
   She does not stop what she is doing to talk to me. She continues whatever she is involved in, such as washing the dishes. She will not look at me: and she is very good at the 'broken record' in that she will keep on repeating: 'A few sweets on occasions will not do the child any harm'!

6. (A) and (B) then act out the role-play, with (A) behaving as he would normally do with his mother.

7. Afterwards, group members give (A) feedback as to the appropriateness of his verbal and non-verbal behaviour, and make suggestions as to how he might change it, e.g.:
   It might help if you didn't just rush straight into the issue. You could start by asking your mother if she would like a cup of coffee. Suggest you both sit down for a while to drink it. Then, try to remain calm and in control. In the role play, you sounded aggressive from the beginning, and you could see that you were getting your mother's back up right from the beginning.

8. It can help to reverse roles, e.g.: (A) could take the role of his mother, and either (B) or another group member should take (A)'s role. In this way, (A) gets the opportunity to observe an alternative way of dealing with the situation.

9. After further discussion, (A) can do the scene again, this time incorporating the new verbal and non-verbal behaviours.

10. Finally, the group can discuss what they have learned from doing and observing the role-play, what difficulties it raises, what factors create blocks to being appropriately assertive in different situations, etc.

11. (A) should take with him an 'Action Plan' as to how he will now deal with that situation.

Further Reading

Back, K. and Back, K. (1986) *Assertiveness at Work*. McGraw-Hill.

Dickson, A. (1982) *A Woman in Your Own Right*. Quartet Books Limited.

Jeffers, S. (1987) *Feel the Fear and Do it Anyway.* Arrow Books Limited.

Lamplugh, D. (1988) *Beating Aggression*. Weidenfield Paperbacks.

Lindenfield, G. (1986) *Assert Yourself*. Thorsons Publishers Limited.

Maddux, R. (1988) *Successful Negotiation*. Kogan Page.

Nelson-Jones, R. (1986) *Human Relationship Skills*. Holt, Rinehart and Winston Ltd.

Module 4: Giving and Receiving Feedback

? Aim

To develop further knowledge and skills in relation to being assertive.

◎ Objectives

1. To discuss giving and receiving critical and positive feedback as an aspect of assertive behaviour.
2. To practise giving and receiving critical feedback.
3. To practise giving and receiving positive feedback.
4. To identify ways in which assertive behaviour could be integrated in to practice within the unit.

▣ Structure of Module

1. Input by Group Leader: Giving and Receiving Feedback
2. Exercise 4.1: Critical Feedback
3. Input by Group Leader: Framework for Giving and Receiving Critical Feedback
4. Exercise 4.2: Giving and Receiving Critical Feedback
5. Exercise 4.3: Framework for Giving and Receiving Positive Feedback
6. Exercise 4.4: Developing an Action Plan
7. Further Reading

✎ Materials Required

Flipchart, pens, blu-tack; A4 paper and pens or pencils.
Copies of handouts:

- *Giving Critical Feedback*
- *Receiving Critical Feedback*
- *Team Action Plan*

◻ Input by Group Leader: Giving and Receiving Feedback

Use this text verbatim, if wished:

❝ If members of a team are to work effectively with each other, it is important that people are able to state what they think and feel without fear of a negative response. The importance of being able to share difficulties with others has been acknowledged as a means of managing stress. However, this presupposes a level of openness and trust, which teams need to develop. Similarly, if team members are to resolve problems, it is often necessary to confront them honestly and squarely with the people concerned. This, if done appropriately, creates a more healthy atmosphere than talking about someone 'behind their back'.

Giving critical feedback directly to the person concerned is far from an easy process. Taken along a continuum, the ideal situation is to always directly confront the person involved; the least desirable situation is not telling the person directly. The aim of the next two exercises is to look at issues involved in giving and receiving critical feedback in a constructive way, and to have practice in developing this skill. ❞

✓ Exercise 4.1: Critical Feedback

❓ Purpose   To explore the consequences of not giving critical feedback.

👥 Method   Participants in groups of 3–4.
Large group feedback.

🕐 Time   20–30 minutes (10–15 minutes in small group; 10–15 minutes
in large group).

✏️ Materials Flip chart paper and pens, blu-tack, A4 paper and pens or
pencils.

➚ Process

1. State the purpose of exercise.
2. Write on the flipchart or whiteboard the following two questions:
   - Why do we find giving **critical** feedback difficult?
   - What are the consequences of not letting someone know when you are
     unhappy about something they have done?
3. Divide participants into small groups to discuss these questions, and ask
   them to make a note of their responses.
4. Participants return to the large group. Ask each small group in turn to state
   a reason why giving critical feedback is difficult. Write their responses on
   flipchart paper, going round the groups until all contributions have been
   made. The flipchart paper should then be put on the wall for all to see
   throughout the remainder of the day.
5. Issues might include:
   - Fear of hurting feelings.
   - Scared that you might not say what you want to say appropriately.
   - Fear of showing yourself up.
   - Scared about possible consequences, especially if speaking out to
     someone in a higher position.
     It is likely that the element of 'fear' will figure largely, either implicitly or
   explicitly. Emphasise that this negative feeling can act as a real block, and can
   prevent communication.
6. Similarly, ask each group in turn to state a consequence of not giving critical
   feedback. Again, write their responses on flipchart paper, and blu-tack to wall.
7. Consequences might include:
   - Nothing changes.
   - Issues become bigger, issues fester, and create more stress.
   - Issues affect your work and your whole life.
   - A cycle is created which causes increasingly negative feelings.
   - Issues can cause isolation: i.e. withdrawal from situation or other people.
   - Issues can cause group breakdown: break into different factions, cliques,
     etc.
   - Bad practice developing, as teamwork is affected: service users suffer!

8. It is useful to place emphasis on the fact that ultimately, it is the client, the user of the services who suffers. This can then be used as an incentive to staff to really tackle the problem of giving or receiving critical feedback in a constructive way. It can help them understand that there is a strong ethical dimension to tackling this issue and combating their identified 'fears'.

Input by Group Leader: Framework for Giving and Receiving Critical Feedback

Purpose   To enable participants to understand how critical feedback can be given and received in a constructive way.

Method   Handouts, with clarification by group leader as required.

Time   10 minutes.

Materials Handouts: *Giving Critical Feedback*
                         Receiving Critical Feedback

Process

1. Give out handout *Giving Critical Feedback*. Read through it with the group, giving opportunity for questions to be asked.
2. Repeat this process with handout *Receiving Critical Feedback*.

Exercise 4.2: Giving and Receiving Critical Feedback

Purpose   To give participants the opportunity to practise giving and receiving critical feedback, using appropriately assertive verbal and non-verbal behaviour.

Method   Participants in groups of 3–4.
Large group feedback.

Time   1–1¼ hours.

Materials   None.

Note to Group Leader: This is an extremely sensitive exercise, and should be managed with care. It should not be undertaken at all if you have little experience of working with groups of people, and find it difficult to key in to the atmosphere or dynamics of a group. It is important to be sensitive to what is happening to individuals within the group, and to be able to identify and deal with any issues that may come up, including conflicts that have been festering for some time! If you are not a manager within the staff team, nor well acquainted with its members, it is important that you liaise with the unit leader, to identify how any issues can be picked up and responded to as necessary.

If the situation does not seem to be conducive to carrying out this exercise 'for real', or you feel unsure of your ability to manage it appropriately, it may be preferable for you to ask participants to 'role-play' situations, introducing issues that they would like to deal with, but which do not directly involve anyone in the group. In this case, the process would be the same, except for the fact that the person on the receiving end of the critical feedback would have to be given sufficient information to 'step into the shoes' of the other person. Despite this 'health warning', it is relevant to say that generally people choose to feedback at a level that can be handled within the group, and it is only rarely that a difficult situation is created. More usually, issues have been resolved, and often, so have long-existing misunderstandings!

Process

1. State the purpose of the exercise, and explain in detail what they are going to do, before they divide into groups.
2. Acknowledge that this is not an easy exercise. However, in order to develop the skill, it is important to get practice in a 'protected' setting. Point out again the value of improving this skill, in terms of its ultimate effects on the staff team and on service users if it is not acquired.
3. Explain that each person is to give each member of their group feedback in terms of the following:

One thing I would like you to have done, or to do, differently or less, or more is:

Emphasise that they should use the guidelines laid down in the handouts to the last exercise to help them frame what they say, and to think about communicating in an assertive way, in terms of their verbal and non-verbal behaviour.

4. The person receiving the feedback is to respond, again using the guidelines suggested in the handout.
5. This should lead to a discussion of the issue, and if possible, a resolution.
6. The other people should act as observers. After the dialogue is completed, the observers should give feedback in terms of how appropriately they felt the issue was dealt with. Again, they can use the points raised in the handout to structure their comments. Also, feedback can be given in relation to verbal and non-verbal behaviour, as covered in the previous session on Assertiveness.
7. Emphasise that the actual content of what is said in the small group will remain confidential to that group. Later, the large group will focus in the main on the feelings raised by undertaking this exercise.
8. Now, divide into small groups. The Group Leader should not be involved in any group, but should check with each group after a few minutes that they are clear about what they are doing, and feel all right about it.
9. After about 45 minutes, ask participants to return to the large group. Discuss how they felt about doing this exercise—what made it difficult, and what was helpful.
10. Consideration should then be given as to how people can be encouraged to give each other direct critical feedback, rather than talk to a third person: which can be seen as 'gossiping', 'backbiting' or 'bitching'. This is not conducive to a pleasant working environment, and each person has a responsibility to ensure that it does not happen. One means of doing this is to suggest that the team establishes a 'group contract', i.e. that each person commits themselves to not accepting critical feedback about a third person. So, for example, if A talks to B about C, then B suggests that A should either give the feedback directly to C; or alternatively, not say anything at all. If everyone within a staff team commits themselves to doing this, then 'behind the back' complaining or gossiping soon ceases. Team members are in effect agreeing to monitor each other as well as themselves.
11. It can be beneficial to have a coffee or lunch break after completion of this exercise.

✓ Exercise 4.3: Framework for Giving and Receiving Positive Feedback

? Purpose To enable participants to practise giving and receiving positive feedback.

👥 Method Formal input by Group Leader.
Groups of 3–4.
Large group feedback.

🕐 Time 30–45 minutes.

✏️ Materials None.

↗ Process

1. The Group Leader starts off by saying something along these lines:

❝ We are now going to look at compliments, to show that assertiveness is about expressing positive feelings and ideas as well as negative ones. Many people feel awkward about giving and receiving compliments. When saying something positive, it is important to be clear and specific, e.g.:

   'That is a lovely coat',

or,

   'I was very impressed by what you said at the meeting'.

When receiving a compliment, do not try to deflect it. For example, if someone says:

   'That is a nice dress'

do not respond with,

   'Oh, I have had this one for ages!'

or if a visitor comments on the fact that they like your choice of wallpaper, do not be tempted to put yourself down by suggesting that you have not really got very good taste. If we insist on responding to our own embarrassment by rejecting the compliment, we succeed in making the other person feel devalued, and wishing that they had not made the effort to give you some praise. Both people end up feeling not very good in a situation which should actually leave everyone involved feeling positive!

   To be assertive, you should accept, acknowledge, and if appropriate, agree with a compliment. For example:

   'That was a lovely meal'. 'Thank you very much, I am pleased with how it turned out.'

or:

   'You spoke up well at that meeting'. 'I am glad you thought so. I felt nervous before I started, but I am pleased that I came across well.' ❞

2. Tell participants that they are now to be given the opportunity to compliment each other in turn within small groups. They can give **positive** feedback in one of two areas:

- Some skill the other person has e.g. playing the piano, communicating with children.
- Something the other person has said or done, e.g., 'I really appreciated when you stayed behind to help me in that difficult situation with Robert: I was frightened, and you supported me'.

Emphasise that all compliments should be genuine! Everyone has positive qualities, and it is important within staff teams to recognise and build on these. Thus, even between individuals who personally dislike each other, it is important to become more consciously aware of each other's positive characteristics. Compliments should be accepted and acknowledged assertively!

3. Divide into groups of 4–5: these groups should consist of different people to those who worked together in the previous exercise. Every person in the group should give every other person some positive feedback.

4. After 15–20 minutes, return to the large group. Have a brief discussion as to how this felt. People tend to find it easier than being critical. Although there may be feelings of embarrassment expressed, there is generally a high degree of pleasure involved in the process. On occasions, deep emotion can be stirred, if someone receives appreciative feedback that was particularly significant for them.

5. To round off this session, it is worthwhile pointing out that, because of the embarrassment we experience, we tend to avoid telling people when we appreciate them, even those who are closest to us. Hence, people do not always get to know what we feel. For many, this can have adverse consequences, in that they lose someone close, and there is a regret that 'I never told them how much I cared about them'.

Suggest that each individual identifies one person in their mind, either in or out of the work situation, whom they feel positively about, and commits themselves to telling that person what it is they appreciate!

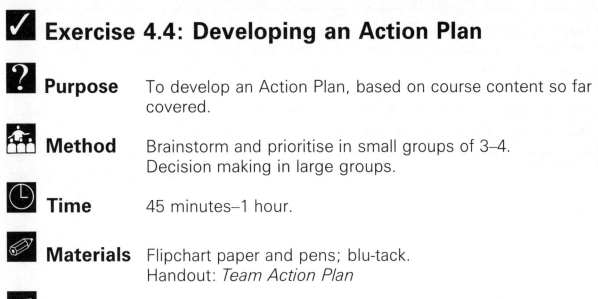

✓ Exercise 4.4: Developing an Action Plan

? Purpose To develop an Action Plan, based on course content so far covered.

Method Brainstorm and prioritise in small groups of 3–4.
Decision making in large groups.

🕓 Time 45 minutes–1 hour.

Materials Flipchart paper and pens; blu-tack.
Handout: *Team Action Plan*

↗ Process

1. State the purpose of the exercise and explain what is to happen.
2. Ask people to divide into small groups. In their groups, they are to review the course content covered in the four modules.
3. Each group should identify a 'scribe'. For the first few minutes, group members should brainstorm different ways in which the learning gained from the Programme could be used in practice. As many ideas as possible should be noted, including ones which individuals feel have not much chance of being implemented. For example, one suggestion might be:
   'At the end of each staff meeting, we should all spend ten minutes doing a relaxation exercise' or 'the first 10 minutes of each handover meeting will be used to give people the opportunity to off-load feelings, without being judged or condemned for what they feel'.
4. After the brainstorming is completed, the group should review what has been written, and prioritise four items which they wish to bring to the large group. These should be written on a separate sheet of flipchart paper. This paper should then be put on the wall, or in some place where all can see them.
5. Each alternative should be explained and discussed in the large group, with any queries or possible modifications to the suggestions being debated.
6. Each individual should then decide which four of the suggestions are most valid, and should take priority in being implemented. When everyone has noted their own choice, the group leader should go round the group, asking each person to identify what their choices are, and placing a tick beside the relevant suggestions on the flipchart paper.
7. When everyone's vote has been recorded, the suggestion that has the greatest number of ticks beside it is the first agreed 'goal' which the group should aim to achieve.
8. An Action Plan should then be drawn up, using the handout *Team Action Plan* as a framework for discussion and decision making.
9. This handout should be filled in by each person individually, or one copy completed, with photocopies made and distributed as soon as possible.

Note to Group Leader: Should more than one goal be identified, then a different sheet should be completed for each goal. However, it is best to select only one, and be sure that it is achieved, rather than to be too ambitious, and attempt to undertake too much change at one time. After the first goal has been effectively accomplished, then the same process can be carried out with the suggestion given second priority.

📄 Handout: Giving Critical Feedback

Acknowledge the Positive

Although the aim is to give critical feedback, it is helpful if this can be done within a context which first acknowledges some positive factor that is relevant to the current situation. For example:

> *Usually, I feel you relate well to Stephen. However, this morning, when you were wanting him to get up, I felt that you did not give him sufficient time to waken, and were inappropriately angry with him.*

Be Specific

It is important to be very clear about what it is you are saying, and not to be too generalised in your comments. For example, in the above situation, you might expand what you mean by continuing:

> *You were shouting loudly, and came across as being very aggressive.*

Focus on Behaviour that can be Changed

There is no value in giving people feedback which appears to condemn them as a person. Avoid statements such as:

> *You really haven't got a clue how to relate to children.*

Remain Calm

Giving critical feedback is not easy. It is important to retain control over your behaviour, and not become either aggressive in your approach, or too nervous to communicate effectively. Remember to keep appropriate eye contact, and an even tone of voice. It can help to practice what you are going to say beforehand.

Keep to the Point

If the person on the receiving end of the feedback becomes actively defensive, they may well respond by attacking you in some way. Ensure that you stay with the situation you have raised, using the 'broken record' technique to help you if necessary. For example:

> *I understand that you consider I was largely responsible for the row that arose between Tom and Lisa last night. If you wish, we can talk about that later. However, at the moment, I really want to discuss the situation that arose with Stephen this morning.*

Do not put People Down, or use Stereotypical Labels

For example, avoid comments such as:

> *You're a typical woman . . .*
> *. . . male chauvinist pig . . .*

▣ Handout: Receiving Critical Feedback

Avoid a Defensive Response

It is very easy to respond in a negative way to any feedback that has an element of criticism in it, and to become defensive. Try to avoid a response of this nature, remain calm, and actively listen to what is being said.

Determine Whether the Criticism is Specific or General

If the criticism is general, ask the person to be more specific about what they are saying. For example:

> *You have said that I am slovenly. Can you give me an example of what I have done which leads you to think this about me?*

Determine Whether you Agree With the Criticism or Not

Think carefully about what has been said. If you can agree with it, acknowledge what has been said, and make a relevant response. For example:

> *I can accept that my entries in the logbook are rather lengthy, I am not good at writing briefly and clearly, and am hoping soon to go on a Report Writing course.*

If you do not agree with the criticism, say so assertively. For example:

> *I do not agree that I was not strict enough with Karen last night. She apologised for being late, and gave me a good reason for being so, so I did not feel that it was necessary to sanction her.*

Challenge Put-downs

For example, an assertive response to someone who states that you made a 'crazy decision' might be:

> *I do not accept that it was a crazy decision. It may not have been the wisest decision under the circumstances, but it was what I felt to be in the best interests of everyone concerned at the time.*

Acknowledge Constructive Criticism

If someone has given you constructive critical feedback, it can be helpful to acknowledge the fact that this may have been difficult to do. For example:

> *I am glad that you felt able to say what you have done. I realise that it is not an easy thing to do, but I have found it useful.*

▣ Handout: Team Action Plan

1. What is our agreed goal?

2. In order to achieve our goal, what needs to be done? (Make a list of all tasks.)

3. Who is going to be responsible for ensuring that each of the identified tasks are undertaken? (Different people can be identified for different tasks.)

4. What factors might help us to achieve our goal?

5. What factors might hinder us achieving our goal?

6. How can we increase helping factors?

7. How can we lessen the influence of hindering factors?

8. When will we review progress on what has been agreed? (For example, it may be decided to put it on the staff meeting agenda in three months time.)

9. Who is to take responsibility for ensuring that the agreed action plan is implemented? (This need not be a person who is actually involved in implementing the action plan.)

Further Reading

Back, K. and Back, K. (1986) *Assertiveness at Work*. McGraw-Hill.
Dickson, A. (1982) *A Woman in Your Own Right*. Quartet Books Limited.
Jeffers, S. (1987) *Feel the Fear and Do it Anyway*. Arrow Books Limited.
Lamplugh, D. (1988) *Beating Aggression*. Weidenfield Paperbacks.
Lindenfield, G. (1986) *Assert Yourself*. Thorsons Publishers Limited.

Module 5: Values into Practice

? Aim

To establish how the values and principles held by team members affect their practice, and to identify ways of evaluating practice based on an agreed set of principles.

◎ Objectives

1. To develop understanding of the terms 'values' and 'principles'.
2. To identify values held by members of the team.
3. To explore the origins of a person's values.
4. To discuss similarities and differences in values held by members of the team, and the implications of these for practice.
5. To establish a set of values and principles that should underpin the work that we do.
6. To begin to explore the implications of translating values and principles into practice, based on 'reflective practice'.
7. To draw up a team agenda which identifies issues that need addressing within the team.

🁢 Structure of Module

1. Input by Group Leader: Values and Principles
2. Exercise 5.1: What Do We Believe?
3. Exercise 5.2: Sharing Values and Beliefs
4. Exercise 5.3: Values into Practice
5. Exercise 5.4: Setting a Team Agenda

✎ Materials Required

Flipchart, pens, blu-tack, A4 paper, pens or pencils.

Copies of handouts:
- *Exercise in Values*
- *Are We Always Right in What We Believe?*

☐ Input by Group Leader: Values and Principles

Use this text verbatim, if wished:

❛The aim of this session is to understand more clearly the terms 'values' and 'principles', and to find out more about how they influence what happens on a day-to-day level. An initial exercise may help illustrate the significance of values.❜

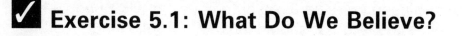

✓ Exercise 5.1: What Do We Believe?

? Purpose   To highlight differences in values and beliefs held by members of the staff team and to begin to explore reasons why these differences exist.

Method   Completion of trigger sentences by individuals.
Feedback to large group and discussion.

Time   20–30 minutes.

Materials   Flipchart or white board, paper and pens or pencils.

Process

1. Ensure that everyone has paper, and pen or pencil.
2. Put the following phrases up on the flipchart or white board:
   - Religion is _____
   - Women are _____
   - Children should _____
   - Black people are _____
   - A family consists of _____
   - The purpose of life is _____
   - I believe that _____
   - The person who has influenced me most in my life is _____
3. Ask each person to complete these sentences in whatever way they choose. Encourage them to do so as spontaneously as possible.
4. When all have finished, take one phrase at a time, and ask people to read out in turn what they have written. At this stage, no one should comment, and everyone should listen, and note similarities and differences.

Note to Group Leader: It may be helpful to have a different person starting the round on each occasion, so that the same person does not always start first.

---

5. Ask people for their responses to what they have heard. Generally, there will be substantial differences in what has been said. For example, 'Religion is . . .' may include the following variations:
   - 'Religion is a belief in God'.
   - 'Religion is a load of mumbo-jumbo'.
   - 'Religion is the opium of the people'.
   'Women are . . .' may include:
   - 'Women are caring'.
   - 'Women are individuals'.
   - 'Women are equal to men'.

6. Encourage a discussion as to why there are differences in what people have written. The main points to bring out should include the following:

- The way we complete these sentences reflects the beliefs that we have. Our beliefs are to a great extent determined by the way we were brought up, and by the attitudes and values that we were encouraged to hold by significant people in our life. In other words, beliefs and values are passed on by other human beings (who like any other human being may be mistaken in what they think), rather than necessarily representing an 'absolute truth'. Hence, we need to view all our beliefs in a critical way, questioning whether or not they are valid.

- Refer to the last phrase, 'the person who has influenced me most in my life is . . .' Very often, people select mother, father, or another person who was significant in childhood. Those beliefs that were fed into us as children are the most difficult to challenge, as they are the most deep-rooted. Because they are instilled in us at such a deep level, we often do not realise that what we perceive as 'fact' or 'common-sense' is in fact an indoctrinated belief. Until we understand what our own individual values are, and from where we have acquired them, we are psychological 'prisoners' of someone else's teaching and ideas. We have not fully taken the opportunity to develop a set of beliefs and values that are totally our own.

  People's values are like their kidneys; they rarely know they have any until they are upset'

  This issue is raised again in more depth in Exercise 2.

- Often, people avoid completing the phrase 'children should . . .' by 'children should be seen and not heard'. There is a general realisation that this is an inappropriate view to hold. However, it is worth asking how people in wider society might respond to that phrase. There is usually a recognition that we live in a society where that belief is widely held, suggesting that children have less rights than adults.

✓ Exercise 5.2: Sharing Values and Beliefs

❓ Purpose   To develop understanding of the terms 'values' and 'principles'.
To gain the opportunity to share differences in beliefs held.
To explore the reasons for those differences.

Method   Formal input.
Exercise in small groups of 4–5.
Large group discussion.

🕐 Time   35–45 + minutes.

✏️ Materials   Handouts: *Exercise in Values*
Are We Always Right in What We Believe?

↗ Process

1. Formal input by Group Leader; use verbatim if wished:

   ❝ It is important to have a clear understanding of what we mean by the term 'values'. A dictionary definition is that 'values' are 'principles which guide action'. An alternative way of phrasing this might be that values are 'principles or beliefs that influence our behaviour'.

   It is helpful to increase our understanding on a conscious level about what beliefs we have, how they influence our behaviour and from where we have gained these beliefs. One way of doing this is to share and compare our views with others. ❞

2. Give out handout *Exercise in Values*. Divide the team into small groups of 3 or 4 to respond to each of these questions for 20–30 minutes. One person in each group to record the main points of similarity and difference.
3. Feedback into large group. Points to make:
   - We have been sharing the beliefs that we carry.
   - Beliefs are fed into us from birth.
   - We see many of them as 'common-sense': i.e. common to us, but they may not necessarily be so to others.
   - We need to look at them critically, in an objective way. Why do I believe this? What evidence have I got that I am right, and others are wrong?
   - No human being has access to the 'ultimate truth'.
4. Handout *Are We Always Right in What We Believe?* can be distributed. Participants can either be given the opportunity to read this and ask questions; or to retain it for reading after the formal training session.

5. Concluding input by Group Leader:

❝ If we are to be members of an effective team, then we need to clarify the values that we hold, and examine the implications of these for practice. Unless we are able to reach agreement on these, then each of us is going to behave according to a differing set of values, some of which may actually be in conflict with each other. If I believe that 'we decide what service is to be offered', and you believe that 'the service we offer needs to be flexible to meet the needs of the user', then we are each going to respond differently to users. What they will experience is inconsistency. We as a staff group need to consider, fully discuss, and find some means of resolving these issues if those that we work with are to receive a good service. ❞

✓ Exercise 5.3: Values into Practice

? Purpose   To identify an agreed set of values and principles that should give the basis for providing a quality service.

Method   Exercises in small groups.
Feedback and discussion in large group.

Time   1–1 ½ + hours.

Materials   Paper and pens.

Process

1. Divide into small groups, and ask participants to brainstorm what they consider to be appropriate values to underpin the professional practice of the team. These could include, for example:
   - **Equality**
     The principle of equality is based on the belief that **all** human beings are equal based on their shared humanity, regardless of race, gender, class, sexuality, age, disability, religion, or culture.
   - **Individuality**
     The principle of individuality is based on the belief that each human being is a unique person, with an equal right to have their individuality recognised and acknowledged.
   - **Choice**
     The principle of choice is based on the belief that all people have the right to participate in the making of decisions which affect their lives.
   - **Capacity for Change**
     The principle of change is based on the belief that everyone has capacity for constructive change and development.
2. When they have identified as many as they feel to be relevant, the group should then determine those which they feel to be most significant (maximum of six).
3. For each value, group members should identify three of four specific implications for practice, e.g.:
   Equality
   - *All people, whatever their age and abilities, have an equal right to express their needs, wants and feelings.*
   - *All people have a right to have their needs acknowledged and responded to on an equal basis to all others; which means that the exercising of one person's rights should not be to the detriment of others.*
   Individuality
   - *The aim should be to ensure that the individual needs of each person are identified and met, including spiritual, physical, intellectual, cultural, emotional and social needs.*

Choice

- *All people have the right to participate in determining their own futures.*
- *All people should be enabled to have the opportunities to make choices in relation to all aspects of their daily lives.*
- *All people have the right to make mistakes, and to learn from their mistakes.*
- *All people have the right to privacy.*

Capacity for Change

- *All people should be given the opportunity to recognise that constructive change and development is possible.*
- *Each person should be encouraged to see that change can be a positive factor in their lives, and be enabled to experience it as such.*
- *Each person should have access to opportunities that will enable them to develop their potential in a planned and purposeful way.*

4. Each group should then feed back the result of their discussions into the large group.

5. Ideally, the outcome of this exercise should be typed up and distributed to each team member, if someone is prepared to take responsibility for doing so. It is then worthwhile reconsidering it at periodic intervals, to review whether, in the light of practice, there needs to be additions or modifications.

✓ Exercise 5.4: Setting a Team Agenda

? Purpose To enable staff to identify issues which they feel would benefit from being addressed within the staff team.

Method Brainstorming in pairs.
A decision-making process taking place in small and large groups.

🕐 Time 45–60 minutes.

✏️ Materials Small and large sheets of paper, pens and blu-tack.

↗ Process

1. In pairs, discuss issues, concerns, problems, etc., that you would like to work on within the team. These can be on any level, and may include issues generating out of the previous exercise, e.g.:
   - We do not give service users adequate opportunity to state what they wish to happen.
   - We have not addressed issues of racism or sexism sufficiently in this team.
   - We should develop better ways of dealing with feelings within the team.
   - Not everyone's skills are sufficiently used in this team.
   - We are not kept in touch with what is happening higher in the organisation.
   - We do not pay sufficient attention to personal development issues.
2. Each issue to be written on a piece of paper.
3. Move into groups of four. Issues should be shared, identifying those held in common. Issues that have strong similarities should be re-written on a larger sheet of paper.
4. Display all pieces of paper on a table or wall.
5. Some time should be given to enable people to look at what has been written. Each person should tick four or five issues they feel are most significant for them.
6. Those items having the greatest number of ticks are the issues that should be given priority to be addressed within the team. Inform staff that you will use some of these in future modules as part of the training process, when looking at making effective use of meetings, and staff supervision.

> Note to Group Leader: Again, work carried out in this exercise will be used later in the Programme. Issues identified by the staff group should be typed out in order of priority. Copies can be distributed to all staff in the form of a handout, with the request that they retain it for future reference.

◪ Handout: Exercise in Values

On your own:

1. Look back to your childhood. Identify what you were encouraged to believe in each of the following areas:
   - Religion

   _____

   _____

   - Education

   _____

   _____

   - Role of women

   _____

   _____

   - Role of men

   _____

   _____

   - Behaviour of children

   _____

   _____

   - Black people

   _____

   _____

   - Sexual relationships

   _____

   _____

2. Who influenced you in the beliefs that you held?
3. Have your beliefs changed in any of these areas? If so, can you identify:

   (a) In what ways your beliefs have changed?
   (b) What or who has influenced you in your change of beliefs?

📄 Handout: Are We Always Right in What We Believe?

As individuals, the more we insist that the beliefs we hold are completely 'right', the less freedom we have to modify and change them. The more we see that the beliefs we hold are in fact only structures of our own making, with no guarantee that they represent the 'truth', then the greater insecurity we may feel. However, if we have the knowledge that our beliefs are created by ourselves, then we are free to change them.

The need to see our beliefs as 'right' can blind us to the fact that other people see things in different ways. This can lead us to think that anyone who perceives things differently from us is either mad or bad, or perhaps both. The way we experience our existence is so basic to our understanding of what life is about, we often assume that everyone else sees their existence in the same way as we do. This assumption lies at the root of most disagreements and conflict between people.

It takes courage to accept and to live in the knowledge that we are in a world which we have made. It means accepting not only uncertainty but also responsibility. It means accepting what Kierkegaard called 'the anguish of Abraham'. Abraham obeyed the voice of the angel who bade him sacrifice his son Isaac. But even in the act of such obedience, it was Abraham who made the decision to interpret the voice he heard as that of an angel from God, and not as a tempting devil or an hallucination.

It takes courage to live with uncertainty and responsibility. However, the alternatives, though seeming on the face of it to be more attractive, may in the end result in greater damage. If we insist that our construction of reality is the true and only one, we condemn ourselves to a restricted understanding of life. If we try to force other people to take the same view, then we are condemning both them and ourselves.

We may claim that our version of reality is the 'truth', so that we can gain security from the belief that we have chosen the right way, and that others who do not believe the same way are wrong. Or we can recognise that our beliefs are always open to question. If we accept that our construction of reality is created by ourselves, and that each person has created their own reality, then we have to live with the uncertainty of not knowing how 'real' our reality is.

We can choose to define that uncertainty as either a prison or freedom. We can feel threatened by insecurity. Or we can experience life as an exciting adventure, where we constantly have the opportunity to develop our ideas and beliefs in the light of new experiences. We can also learn through listening to other people's stories, and by doing so, reach a better understanding of their perception of reality. In this way, communication at a real level develops; relationships reflect tolerance and acceptance.

Further Reading

Banks, S. (2001) *Ethics and Values in Social Work*. Palgrave, formerly
  Macmillan Press.

Module 6: Effective Use of Meetings

❓ Aim

To enable staff to make more effective use of meetings.

◎ Objectives

1. To share feelings on how team members perceive meeting time to be currently used.
2. To explore the advantages and disadvantages of making decisions as a team rather than on an individual basis.
3. To identify skills required in managing an effective meeting.
4. To hold a meeting which focuses on issues placed on the Team Agenda.

🗂 Structure of Module

1. Exercise 6.1: Review of Previous Sessions
2. Input by Group Leader: Introduction to 'Meetings'
3. Exercise 6.2: Making Effective Use of Meetings
4. Exercise 6.3: Decision-Making in Teams: NASA Moon Landing Exercise
5. Exercise 6.4: The Team Agenda
6. Exercise 6.5: Agreeing the Team Action Plan
7. Further Reading

✏️ Materials Required

Flipchart, pens, A4 paper, pens and pencils.

Copies of handouts:
- *Team Action Plan* (as completed at the end of Module 4)
- *How is Meeting Time Used in Your Team?*
- *Making Effective Use of Meetings*
- *Moon Landing Exercise: Instructions*
- *Moon Landing Exercise: Answer Key*
- *Team Work Questionnaire*

Copy of 'Team Agenda' drawn up during Module 5 (Exercise 5.4).

✓ Exercise 6.1: Review of Previous Sessions

Note to Group Leader: This initial exercise is not necessary to the content of the rest of the day. However, it is useful to encourage participants to review what has so far happened on the course, in order to reinforce what has been previously learnt, and to encourage people to continue to make connections between course content, and what is happening in practice.

? Purpose   To review what has happened on the course to date.
To evaluate progress on the Team Action Plan drawn up at the end of Module 4.

Method   Discussion in pairs, then feedback in large group.

🕐 Time   30–45 minutes.

Materials   Handout: *Team Action Plan* (as completed at the end of Module 4)

↗ Process

1. Ask participants to review (in pairs) what has happened on the Programme during the previous sessions. People should be encouraged to refer to their handouts as a means of 'memory recall'.
2. After this review, partners should share with each other what they have found particularly useful and not useful. Each person should identify at least one main learning point which they feel they can feed back to the whole group.
3. After about 15 minutes, bring the large group together again. Ask for a volunteer to start by feeding back a main learning point, or something they feel has been gained from the programme. If appropriate, this can be used as a focus for discussion by the group; or simply acknowledged, passing on to the next person.
4. When everyone has had the opportunity to feed back, refer to the Team Action Plan that was agreed in Module 4. Has it been achieved? If not, why not? Using the handout *Team Action Plan* to provide a framework for discussion, identify the factors that have helped or hindered the process of change.
5. Agree anything that needs to be done to enable this particular goal to be achieved. If it has been fully achieved, move on to the next area that was prioritised in the Action Planning process, again following the framework given in the handout.

Note to Group Leader: This last part can be left till the end of the day, if wished.

⬛ Input by Group Leader: Introduction To 'Meetings'

Use this text verbatim, if wished:

❝ The role of meetings in providing a forum where clear communication can take place is a crucial one. In previous sessions, we have looked at a number of reasons why we need to communicate more effectively (e.g. to provide each other with information and support, as a means of lessening the stress that we experience, and to identify and agree a clear value base in order that we can develop agreed working practices). We have also identified and practised skills that improve our methods of communication (i.e. becoming more assertive, in negotiating, handling conflict, and being able to give and receive critical and positive feedback).

To maximise communication between all team members, we need to have the opportunity to meet together as a group, identify what areas require discussion, and ensure the time is sufficiently structured to enable it to be used as efficiently as possible. Formal meetings enable this to occur.

However, it is very easy for meetings to be experienced as unstimulating, boring, and a waste of time. The aim of this session is to assess strengths and weaknesses in current practice, and to agree ways in which our use of meetings can be improved. There is then an exercise which identifies the advantages and disadvantages of working as a team, rather than as isolated individuals. Finally, there is the opportunity to discuss some of the issues identified during the previous session when a 'team agenda' was drawn up. ❞

✓ Exercise 6.2: Making Effective Use of Meetings

? Purpose   To share feelings on how meeting time is currently used.

Method   Completing a questionnaire in pairs (or threes).
Feedback in large group.

🕐 Time   20–35 minutes.

Materials   Flipchart paper and pens.
Handouts: *How Is Meeting Time Used in Your Team?*
Making Effective Use of Meetings

↗ Process

1. Pass round handout *How is Meeting Time Used in Your Team?* Ask participants to divide into pairs for ten minutes, and share feelings on how they feel meeting time is used. Use the questions on the handout to trigger discussion, although it is not necessary to keep rigidly to them. Brief notes should be made on issues discussed.
2. In the large group, gain feedback on each question in turn.

Note for Group Leader: Make a note on flip chart paper of key points raised. List principal meetings; although it should be stated that the main focus in this session is going to be on full staff meetings. It is a principle underlying the Programme that all teams should have meetings with all members present on a regular basis—ideally once a week. If meetings are not held on a regular basis, then this session should be used to demonstrate the value of holding them. As a general rule, meetings should not last longer than 1½–2 hours, as people's concentration span tends not to last beyond that time.

    For each negative point raised, try to encourage people to clarify what is actually happening and why. For example, why is everything discussed not felt to be worthwhile? What is discussed that is not worthwhile, what is worthwhile? Why do we spend too long on some things and not others?

---

3. Ask the group to brainstorm ways in which they could improve meetings that they attend, and write them up on the flipchart.
4. Identify areas of agreement and disagreement.
5. Give out handout *Making Effective Use of Meetings*, and discuss it in the light of the issues that have arisen from the group exercise.
6. Identify specific changes that can be made that will lead to more effective use of meetings.

✓ Exercise 6.3: Decision-Making in Teams: NASA Moon Landing Exercise

? Purpose To explore the advantages and disadvantages of making decisions as a team rather than on an individual basis.
To identify skills involved in enabling effective teamworking.

Method Problem solving exercise undertaken individually and in small groups.

Time 1¾–2 hours.

Materials Handouts: *Moon Landing Exercise: Instructions*
Team Work Questionnaire
Moon Landing Exercise: Answer Key

↗ Process

1. Input from Group Leader: The Role of Staff Meetings

   ❝ Staff meetings give people the opportunity to identify issues that require discussion, and to use the resources of the staff team to advise the best possible outcome in terms of appropriate decision-making.
   The NASA Moon Landing Exercise is one that enables an evaluation of factors influencing the effectiveness of working as a team, and identifies what helps and hinders the teamworking process. ❞

2. Phase 1: Individual Problem Solving
   (a) Ensure that participants have sufficient space to work individually without disturbing others.
   (b) Distribute handout *Moon Landing Exercise: Instructions*. Read through the instructions as printed; stress that this is all the information they have (i.e. do not get drawn into a discussion about the lack of information, etc.) State that initially, each person has ten minutes to complete this exercise **on their own**, without referring or talking to anyone else.
   (c) After clarifying any queries, tell the group when the ten minutes commences. Let them know at the half-way stage, and when two minutes remain. (Should everyone be finished before ten minutes, you can then move on to the next stage).

3. Phase 2: Team Problem Solving
   (a) Inform the group that they are now moving into the second phase, when they are going to work together *as a team*. They are to repeat the same exercise, but this time, they have to determine the order of items **as a team**. (It can be pointed out that there is in fact a set of right answers to this exercise, apparently drawn up by NASA personnel, of which they will later receive a copy).

(b) Divide participants into groups of 4–5 people, and name them Team A, B, etc. Use the room fully so they will disturb each other as little as possible. If practical, different groups should use different rooms.

(c) Highlight that the exercise is completed when the team have reached a decision as to the order of priority that they would give to the 15 items. In reaching a decision within the group, participants should remember what they have learned earlier in the Team Programme: i.e. to state their points of view in an assertive way; not to dominate the group themselves or allow any other person to dominate; and to ensure that everyone has an equal opportunity to have their viewpoint heard, acknowledged and fully taken into consideration.

(d) State that your role is that of time keeper. The groups have a maximum of 40 minutes to complete the task.

(e) Give each team an additional score sheet, marked respectively Team A, Team B, etc., so that the team decision can be recorded. Be careful not to give it to one person—just leave it in the centre of the group: so the team has to make the decision as to who takes or is given the recording role!

(f) Tell the teams when they should start. Do not get drawn into any debate with any group. If appropriate, you can observe 'from a distance' what is happening within each group: but make sure you influence the group dynamics as little as possible.

(g) Give a time check at 20, 30, and 35 minutes. During the last five minutes, place considerable pressure on a group to agree an order if it appears they may not finish on time.

4. Phase 3: Individual Reflection

(a) When all the groups are finished, collect in the team sheets (individuals retain their own responses).

(b) Explain that the next phase is for them to do some individual work for five minutes.

(c) Encourage participants to give themselves enough room to work on their own: they can stay in their team but need to spread out a little more.

(d) Distribute handout *Team Work Questionnaire*. Stress that it is to help them capture what has been happening. It is confidential to them, and will not be collected in.

5. Phase 4: Comparison of Individual and Team Performance

(a) State that now is the opportunity to compare individual and team results. The lower the sum of different scores, the better the individual or team performance.

(b) Distribute handout *NASA Moon Landing Exercise: Answer Key*, and explain carefully the scoring procedure. Each person should write down their own ranking in the second column; then in the third column, the difference between their own answer and the correct one should be recorded. For example, if they put 'box of matches' as number 11, then the difference score would be '4'. Similarly, if their own answer to 'food concentrate' was number 8, then the difference score would again be '4' (i.e. positives and negatives are ignored).

(c) When they have done this, they should add up the sum of their difference scores, and write it in at the foot of the page.

(d) While participants are completing an answer sheet for the responses they made as individuals, the Group Leader should complete an answer sheet for each team.

(e) When everyone has finished, ask each person to read out their individual scores, starting with Team A, then Team B, etc, and write up on flipchart. For each team, find the average individual score: i.e. add up all the scores, then divide by the number of people in the team.

(f) When this has been completed, write the Team Score on the flipchart. Thus, there should be a record of the scores which looks something like the following:

	Team A	Team B
	62	46
	37	65
	49	58
	67	32
	56	48
Total	**271**	**249**
Average score	**54.2**	**49.8**
Group score	**30**	**25**

6. Phase 5: Process of the Group

(a) Using the headings identified in the Handout *Team Work Questionnaire*, lead the discussion either heading by heading, or team by team. (If you observed any of the team processes, use this opportunity to feed back some of your observations on what you saw happening).

(b) At the end of this session, round it off by considering the key questions:
• What behaviours help or hinder team work, i.e. how could we operate more effectively?
• What are the implications for practice?

7. After the exercise has been completed, the following points can be made:

(a) In about 90 per cent of situations, the team score is lower than the average individual score. A creative energy ('synergy') can be generated when a group meet together; i.e. the whole is greater than the sum of its parts.

(b) This energy can be fully used when individuals within the group make constructive use of group dynamics, ensure that everyone's contribution is heard and fully considered and that no-one is allowed to dominate, etc.

(c) When the team score is higher than the average individual score, it is likely that the group process has not been as constructive as it might be. For example, on one occasion, a very dominant male, who had absolutely no knowledge of conditions on the moon, was behaving in a way that suggested that he did, and was aggressively pushing his viewpoint. The other members of the group allowed this to happen. Consequently, the dominant male's extremely high personal score was reflected in the group score.

On another occasion, a member of the group actually had extensive knowledge of conditions on the moon. However, he was a very quiet person, who was not skilled at asserting his ideas. On the two occasions he tried to say something, he was not heard. At no time did any other person actively ask for his point of view.

Every member of the group should take responsibility for ensuring that both they and others are given full opportunity to contribute, but not to dominate.

(d) The advantage of working as a group is that it provides the opportunity for the knowledge and experience of all members of the team to be taken advantage of. The idea of 'synergy' has a chance to positively influence the decision-making process. However, the disadvantage is that it is much more time consuming. In this exercise, individuals had reached a decision within ten minutes; the team took considerably longer to form an agreed response to the same problem. A distinct advantage of reaching decisions as a staff team in the 'real' world of practice is that not only is it likely to be a better decision, but all members of the team will feel they 'own' the outcome. Even if an individual does not agree with the final decision reached, at least they will feel they played a valid role in the process of discussion that took place.

If decisions are imposed on team members, they are less likely to experience this sense of ownership, and hence less likely to implement them in the way that was intended.

(e) In order for this decision-making process to work as effectively as possible, it is crucial that team members place emphasis on structuring their meetings in an appropriate way, and continue to improve their skills in ensuring that all contribute fully and constructively.

✓ Exercise 6.4: The Team Agenda

? Purpose To put knowledge and skills relevant to running a team meeting into practice.

Method Large group exercise.

Time 1¼–2 hours.

Materials Handout: *Making Effective Use of Meetings*

Process

1. Refer to the Team Agenda drawn up in Exercise 5.4 in Module 5 of this Programme. Encourage the team to identify how many items can be addressed within the time available, and which these should be. Generally, it can be useful to start with the issues that were given greatest priority. However, it may be that the team decides to focus on issues further down the list for this exercise.
2. Using the handout *Making Effective Use of Meetings* as a framework, and encourage the team to plan and run the meeting.
3. Suggest that all participants try to play the dual role of being an objective observer of what is going on, as well as being an active participant. As active participant, they should use their own awareness and skills to ensure that the meeting runs constructively, and that all are given the opportunity to contribute, without anyone monopolising. At the same time, as observer, they should be looking out for factors that are either helping or hindering the process of enabling the meeting to be a constructive one for all concerned.
4. The idea of 'Stop the Action' can be introduced, if it is felt to be appropriate, i.e. if someone in their role as 'objective observer' wants to make a positive or critical comment regarding the process, then they can say 'Stop the Action'. The meeting is then suspended, whilst the comment is made and discussed. When this is completed, the meeting starts up again.

> Note to Group Leader: It is important to see this exercise operating at two levels. As the issues are genuine ones, having been identified by team members, and are being discussed by the staff group involved, this is a 'real' situation, rather than a simulated one.
> At the same time, the team are in a training situation, where the emphasis is on acquiring and re-inforcing skills in running and contributing to meetings. Hence, your role is a key one in ensuring that there is as much emphasis placed on being aware of what is happening and reflecting on the processes at work, as much as reaching a decision on the task in hand. The practice of 'Stop the Action' can help this; however, it is important to ensure that this is used in a positive way, and does not develop to a point where it dominates the process of running the meeting.

5. The time spent on evaluating the effectiveness of the meeting at the end should be detailed, and should identify constructive ways of improving practice at further meetings. These should build on suggestions made earlier in the day (Exercise 6.2).

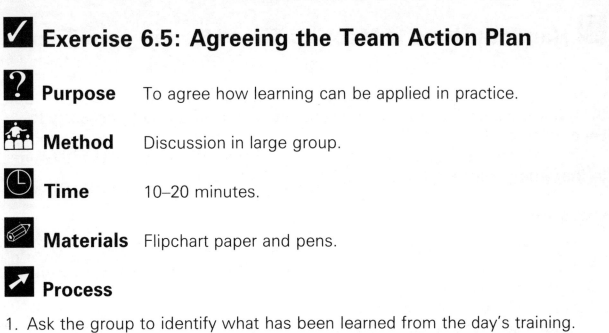

☑ Exercise 6.5: Agreeing the Team Action Plan

? Purpose   To agree how learning can be applied in practice.

Method   Discussion in large group.

Time   10–20 minutes.

Materials   Flipchart paper and pens.

↗ Process

1. Ask the group to identify what has been learned from the day's training. Encourage as many contributions as possible, and write up on the flipchart.
2. Ask for suggestions as to how the learning gained can be applied in practice.

> Note to Group Leader: It may be that this was covered at the end of the previous exercise. If so, then the Action Plan is partially completed. However, agreement has to be made as to how progress is to be evaluated, and who is to take responsibility for ensuring that there is an ongoing emphasis on consciously developing the effective use of meetings.

3. If at the beginning of this Module there were gaps in the review and further planning based on the original Team Action Plan, then this process can now be completed.

▣ Handout: How is Meeting Time Used in your Team?

In pairs, share feelings on how you feel meeting time is used in your team. Use the following questions to trigger discussion, although it is not necessary to keep rigidly to them.

Make brief notes as to the content of your discussion, to feed back afterwards to the large group.

Questions

1. How many different kinds of meetings do we hold?
2. For each kind of meeting, how often do we hold them? What is the average length of each meeting?
3. Is everything we discuss worthwhile?
4. Do we spend too long on some things, and not enough on others?
5. Do you think there are areas we should discuss which are often or always left out?
6. Who decides what is discussed at a meeting? How is this decided and when?
7. Does anyone take formal control as to what happens at the meeting? Is there an agreed chairperson? If so, who is this?
8. How are decisions made? E.g. by manager, other member of team, majority vote, consensus, etc.
9. How do we record what we are doing, and who does this? Where are records of meetings kept? Who has access to them?
10. What happens if the meeting does not seem to be going too well; e.g. when someone feels that we are wasting time, or conflict arises between team members?
11. How much time is spent in meetings sharing how we feel about the work we are doing, or about the nature of the working relationships we have with each other?

⊡ Handout: Making Effective Use of Meetings

There are different types of meetings that can take place within the workplace. These may include full staff meetings, specific task-centred meetings, project review meetings, etc. Whatever the reason for the meeting, there are certain principles and practices that are common to each.

1. **Appointing a chairperson**
   This can be the same person on each occasion (e.g. the manager, team leader, etc.)
   Alternatively, there can be a rotating chairperson. The value of this is that it enables all team members to gain experience and skills in chairing. The role of the chair is to be assertive in ensuring that:
   * Agreed times of the meeting are adhered to, and that no one item takes up substantially more than its allocated time.
   * No one person dominates the discussion.
   * Everyone is encouraged to contribute their views and feelings.
   * The discussion remains relevant to the issue under consideration.
     At the end of each item, the chairperson should summarise what has been covered, and any agreed action.

2. **Establishing time, length and location of meeting**
   Ensure all those who should attend have this information as soon as possible. Meetings should start and end at the agreed time.

3. **Establish purpose of meeting**
   Clarify at the beginning that all those attending are clear about the reason for the meeting being held.

4. **Drawing up a clear agenda**
   This can be done in advance, and circulated to everyone involved, or can be done at the beginning of the meeting. Generally, all intended participants should have the opportunity to contribute to the agenda. Approximate time limits should be allocated to each item, to enable all issues to be covered in the allocated time.

5. **Establishing means of recording meetings**
   Decisions need to be made about:
   * Where meetings are to be recorded.
   * Who is to be responsible for recording them?
   * How much detail is expected in the minutes?
   * Are all decisions to be recorded?
   * Where are the minutes to be kept?

6. **Evaluation of meeting**
   It can be of value to build in five to ten minutes review time at the end of each meeting, to allow people to discuss how useful they have found it. Positive and negative factors can be raised by team members in relation to, for example:

- relevance of issues discussed
- opportunities for all to contribute
- maximising use of time
- appropriateness of atmosphere in encouraging people to share on a feelings level, etc.

Reflection of this nature can act as a learning process, and can help develop understanding as to what can be done to enable more effective use of meetings on future occasions.

▣ Handout: Team Action Plan

What is our agreed goal?

In order to achieve our goal, what needs to be done? (make a list of all tasks).

Who is going to be responsible for ensuring that each of the identifed tasks are undertaken (different people can be identified for different tasks).

What factors might help us to achieve our goal?

What factors might hinder us from achieving our goal?

How can we increase helping factors?

How can we lessen the influence of hindering factors?

When will we review progress on what has been agreed? (For example, it may be decided to put it on the staff meeting agenda in three months time).

Who is to take responsibility for ensuring that the agreed action plan is implemented? (This need not be a person who is actually involved in implementing the action plan).

🖳 Handout: Moon Landing Exercise: Instructions

You are a space crew originally scheduled to rendezvous with a mother ship on the lighted surface of the moon. Due to mechanical difficulties, however, your ship was forced to land at a spot some 200 miles from the rendezvous. During re-entry and landing, much of the equipment aboard was damaged, and, since survival depends on reaching the mother ship, the most critical items available must be chosen for the 200 mile trip. Below are listed the 15 items left intact and undamaged after landing. Your task is to rank them in terms of their importance in allowing your crew to reach the rendezvous point. Place the number 1 by the most important item, the number 2 by the second most important, and so on through to number 15, the least important.

_____   Box of matches

_____   Food concentrates

_____   50 ft. of nylon rope

_____   Parachute silk

_____   Portable heating unit

_____   Two .45 calibre pistols

_____   One case of dehydrated milk

_____   Two 100 lb. tanks of oxygen

_____   Stellar map (of moon's constellation)

_____   Life raft

_____   Magnetic compass

_____   Five gallons of water

_____   Signal flares

_____   First aid kit containing injection needles

_____   Solar-powered FM receiver/transmitter

▣ Handout: Moon Landing Exercise: Answer Key

Item	Reason	NASA Answer	Own Answer	Difference Score
Box of matches	Little or no use	15	____	____
Food concentrates	Supply daily food required	4	____	____
50 ft. of nylon rope	Useful in tying injured together, help in climbing	6	____	____
Parachute silk	Shelter against sun's rays	8	____	____
Portable heating unit	Useful only if party landed on dark side	13	____	____
Two .45 calibre pistols	Self-propulsion devices could be made from them	11	____	____
One case of dehydrated milk	Food mixed with water for drinking	12	____	____
Two 100 lb. tanks of oxygen	Fills respiration requirements	1	____	____
Stellar map (of moon's constellation)	One of principal means of finding directions	3	____	____
Life raft	CO_2 bottled for self-propulsion across chasms, etc.	9	____	____
Magnetic compass	Probably no magnetised poles	14	____	____
5 gallons of water	Replenishes loss by sweating etc.	2	____	____
Signal flares	Distress call when line of sight possible	10	____	____
First aid kit containing injection needles	Oral pills or injection medicine valuable	7	____	____
Solar powered FM receiver/transmitter	Distress signal transmitter, possible communication with mother ship	5	____	____

Sum of Difference Scores = _____

🖳 Handout: Team Work Questionnaire

These questions are designed for your guidance in analysing the effectiveness of your team and the effectiveness of your own performance. Please answer them frankly and with as much detail as you can remember.

1. **Organisation and Planning**
   (a) Did your team spend time planning the task before actually doing it? Was the planning effective?

   How?

   (b) Did the team use time effectively?

   How?

2. **Leadership**
   (a) Was there an appointed leader?

   Who?

   (b) Was there a 'self appointed' leader?

   Who?

   (c) Was there rivalry for leadership?

   Between whom?

3. **Decision Making**
   How were the various decisions made? E.g. by:

   _____   the leader?

   _____   one or two people?

   _____   majority vote?

   _____   consensus?

   _____   unanimity?

4. **Communication**
   (a) Did certain people talk only to each other?

   Who?

   (b) Did some people not talk at all; did it matter?

   Who?

(c) How often was more than one person speaking at once; did it matter?

When?

(d) Was there enough discussion within the team?

When?

5. **Co-operation**
   (a) Did the team members ever stick to their own opinions rather then change them easily?

   Who? When?

   (b) Did the team ever do the job by 'trading' opinions rather than by discussing the facts logically?

   (c) How did the team handle conflict and disagreement between members?

   When?

6. **Individual Performance**
   (a) Were you really satisfied with your contribution?

   (b) How do you think the team saw you?

   (c) What would you do differently in a similar situation?

Further Reading

Woodcock, M. (1979) *Team Development Manual*. Gower.

This includes a number of useful exercises which aim to help assess and improve effectiveness of meetings.

Module 7: Giving and Receiving Support

? Aims

To develop skills in giving and receiving emotional support.
   To introduce the concept of supervision, and to identify its role in providing support.

◎ Objectives

1. To identify what is meant by 'active listening'.
2. To develop understanding of the concept of 'empathy'.
3. To practice empathic responding.
4. To clarify the purpose of supervision.
5. To explore the role of supervision as a means of giving support.

🏠 Structure of Modules

1. Exercise 7.1: Active Listening (1)
2. Exercise 7.2: Active Listening (2)
3. Exercise 7.3: Empathic Listening (1)
4. Exercise 7.4: Empathic Listening (2)
5. Exercise 7.5: Introduction to Supervision
6. Exercise 7.6: Developing Supervision Skills
7. Further Reading

✏️ Materials Required

Flipchart, pens, A4 paper, pens and pencils.

Copies of handouts:
- *Listener's Observer Sheet*
- *Empathic Listening*
- *The Objectives of Supervision*
- *Supervision Modes*
- *Supervision Arrangements*
- *Personal Action Plan*
- *Team Action Plan*

✓ Exercise 7.1: Active Listening (1)

 **Purpose**   To identify the verbal and non-verbal skills involved in active listening.

Method   Exercise in pairs.
Feedback in large group.

Time   15 minutes.

Materials   Flipchart paper and pen.

 **Process**

1. Introduction
   If you are to offer someone support, then it is important that the person to whom you are offering support feels you are actively listening to them. The aim of the following two exercises is to demonstrate what is involved in that process.
2. Ask participants to divide into pairs (A and B), and to sit next to each other.
3. A is to speak to B for two minutes about any subject in which they have an interest e.g. playing golf, listening to music, politics, etc.
4. The aim of B is to do anything but listen! They must remain in the room, but can use any other tactic to avoid listening.
5. After two minutes, ask the group to come together. Discuss what points emerged from this exercise, including:
   * How the listeners were behaving to indicate they were not listening.
   * How the speakers felt about not being listened to.
   * What the Bs might have done to demonstrate that they were in fact listening.
6. As a result of this, write up on flipchart paper examples of behaviour that would show that someone is listening attentively to you. This should include:
   * seating position
   * appropriate eye contact
   * nodding head
   * relaxed body posture
   * suitable facial expressions (generally relaxed and friendly; however, showing concern may also be relevant if the content suggests the other person is upset or sad)
   * suitable verbal responses including 'mm', 'yes', 'I see', etc.

✓ Exercise 7.2: Active Listening (2)

? Purpose   To practise active listening.

Method   Exercise in fours.
Feedback in large group.

Time   30–45 minutes.

Materials   Handout: *Listener's Observer Sheet*

↗ Process

1. Ask each of the pairs in the previous exercise to join up with another pair (A, B, C and D).
2. A and B are to have a five minute conversation in which they discuss what they consider to be the positive and negative aspects about their role within the team.
   Stress that the aim is not to make speeches; each person's task is to talk to and respond to each other, using good verbal and non-verbal listening skills.
3. C and D are observers; they should take notes on A and B's attending and voice-related behaviour. The handout *Listener's Observer Sheet* can be used as a basis for recording feedback.
4. After five minutes, feedback in small groups for five to ten minutes, with speakers saying how they felt in that conversation, and observers sharing their feedback.
5. Repeat exercise with roles reversed, i.e. C and D as speakers, A and B as observers.
6. Return to large group. Ask groups to feed back main points arising from the exercise. Finish by summarising the verbal and non-verbal behaviour involved in active listening. Listening is a powerful way of demonstrating to another person that they are sufficiently valued to be worth the time to be given 'good attention' and responded to in a way that is relevant to their needs. Hence, it is important to be practised in this skill if others are to perceive you as interested in what they say, and hence potentially capable of giving them support when needed.

✓ Exercise 7.3: Empathic Listening (1)

? Purpose   To identify what is meant by 'empathic listening'.

Method   Exercise completed individually.

🕐 Time   10–15 minutes.

✏ Materials   Handout: *Empathic Listening*

↗ Process

1. Ask participants to suggest what they understand the word 'empathy' to mean.
2. Formal input by group leader:

   ❝ One dictionary definition of 'empathy' suggests that it is 'the power of understanding and imaginatively entering into another person's feelings' (*The New Collins Concise English Dictionary*). Thus, it is quite different from 'sympathy', which infers feeling sorry for someone, without necessarily having an awareness of what they are experiencing at an emotional level.

   Empathic listening refers to the ability to be attuned to another's thoughts and feelings, and to be able to communicate this in a way that the other feels understood. Thus, it is a sophisticated skill, which requires a considerable degree of sensitivity and perceptiveness.' ❞

3. Distribute the handout *Empathic Listening*. Ask participants to respond to the questions according to the instructions.
4. When everyone has finished, go through the questions, asking for people's responses, and giving the correct answer when required. As far as possible, ensure that all team members are clear about why the one response demonstrates empathy, whilst the others do not. The correct answers are: 1. (c); 2. (a); 3. (d); 4. (a)

✓ Exercise 7.4: Empathic Listening (2)

? Purpose To practise empathic listening and responding.

Method Exercise in large group.

Time 1/2–1 hour.

Materials Paper and pens.

↗ Process

1. Tell team members that they are now to be involved in an exercise which should enable them to become more skilled in recognising and dealing empathically with another person's feelings and emotions.
2. State that you want them to recall an intense emotional experience (either good or bad) that they would be willing to share with other members of the group, and to write down an account of it as concretely as possible.
3. Emphasise that this should not involve an experience that has or is causing major trauma, e.g. a bereavement, breakdown in a significant relationship, etc. Differentiate between 'top drawer, middle drawer, and bottom drawer' concerns, i.e. top drawer concerns are everyday worries. (Will I catch the bus in time? What will I wear to the party tonight? Will Aston Villa win the match?) Middle drawer concerns are felt at a deeper level, e.g. feeling anxious about the possible outcome of exam results. Bottom drawer concerns represent major life crises, e.g. the death or severe illness of someone close to you. For the purpose of this exercise, a middle drawer concern should be selected.

Note to Group Leader: It is important that this latter point be emphasised. This can be a powerful exercise, especially if a group has gelled and there is a degree of trust. Individuals, if not given prior warning, may select examples of major crises in their lives, thinking they can handle it; they then find that the telling of the situation affects them more deeply than they expected, and they lose emotional control.

Despite this warning, it is important that you as group leader are very aware of how people are dealing with a situation, and are ready to intervene as appropriate. For example, a woman on one course chose to share her experience of her daughter recently leaving home for university, and found that she was more affected by the move than she had been aware. The response on that occasion was to move on fairly quickly, and to pick up the issue on an individual level with the woman concerned at a later stage in the day. In fact, by that stage in the programme, a high degree of support had built up within the team, which this particular participant found she benefited from over the following weeks.

---

4. Before participants write down their own experience, the following can be given as an example:

   I was flying by plane for the first time last year. Everyone re-assured me that it would be all right. It was for the first half hour. Then, without warning, there were a lot of bumps and movement. We had entered a storm, and it felt as if we were being buffeted on a stormy sea. I began to feel very sick. I felt as though we would never get to our destination. I started imagining what I would feel like if the engine failed. I didn't talk to anyone: I just sat as if frozen to the seat, gripping hard on to the sides. My body was totally tense.

5. Ask the group to suggest an empathic response, i.e. a response that might identify the feelings experienced by the person in that situation, and why. An appropriate response might be:

   You were feeling very scared because you feared that the plane might crash in the bad weather, and that you might not survive.

   Ask the group to suggest responses that would clearly not be empathic. Such responses might include:

   - *You shouldn't have been worried. You know that it is safer to fly in a plane than to drive in a car.*
   - *How terrible for you! I wouldn't have been in your shoes for anything!*
   - *You should have taken a drink of whisky. That would have set you up to face anything!*

7. Repeat what you are asking of the group, i.e. that you want each of them to recall an intense emotional experience (either good or bad) that they would be willing to share with other members of the group, and to write down an account of it as concretely as possible. This means that they describe what they did, e.g. gripped hard on the sides of the seat; what they thought, e.g. we will never get to our destination; and what they said, or didn't say, e.g. I didn't talk to anyone. What they should not write down is what they felt, e.g. I felt scared, frightened.

8. When everyone has had the opportunity to finish what they have written, state that you are going to go round the group in turn, ensuring that everyone has the chance to respond to another person's story.

9. Ask for a volunteer to start. Ask that person A to turn to the person next to them B, and read out what they have written. B should demonstrate active listening, and respond empathically.

10. If B has difficulty in reflecting back the feelings, you can suggest that a useful phrase to start with is 'You sound as though you were feeling . . .'

11. After B has had the opportunity to respond, it should be open to other members of the group to give alternative contributions. A should then be asked to identify which responses reflected most closely their own feelings.

12. B then becomes A and turns to the person on their other side, who becomes B. The process is followed as previously.

13. Proceed round the group, with everyone having the opportunity to be both A and B.

Note to Group Leader: You may find one or two people are resistant to writing something down, or are reluctant to be active participants in this exercise. Although they should be encouraged to be directly involved, no one should have too much pressure placed on them to be so.

However, in the latter part of the exercise, those who have chosen not to share an experience should not then be on the receiving end of some-one else's experience. They should, however, keep their position as part of the circle. Thus, they still clearly remain part of the group, although less actively involved for the present.

14. When everyone has read their story, have a general discussion on what people felt about doing that exercise, what learning they gained from it, and how they might apply that learning in practice.
    The following points might be made:
    - The need to be tuned in to people's body language, and to try to identify what people are feeling, even if they do not directly share those feelings verbally. Thus, someone's fairly factual account of a row with a friend or relative may be misleading in terms of how they actually feel about the incident. It may require the listener to respond empathically, before the speaker will feel free to share at a feelings level.
    - This awareness is important when understanding colleagues' behaviour which is causing you stress. Thus, it is easy to interpret another person's behaviour at face value in terms of its immediate negative effects on us. However, it may be important to attempt to understand what is happening to that person which is contributing to them behaving in that way. A trigger question such as 'You look or sound as though you are upset or angry or feeling under pressure ' etc. may be sufficient for a person to talk about something that is causing them concern, or at least, to acknowledge that there are issues which are affecting their behaviour.
    - Awareness of this nature can also increase sensitivity to young people and their families, who may not always be able to verbalise feelings in appropriate ways, or who may believe that no-one can understand how they feel.

✓ Exercise 7.5: Introduction to Supervision

? Purpose   To identify the purpose of supervision.
                  To share previous experience of supervision.

Method   Exercise in groups of 3–4.
                  Large group feedback.

🕐 Time   45 minutes.

✎ Materials   Flipchart paper and pens.
                  Handouts: *The Objectives of Supervision*
                            Supervision Modes
                            Supervision Arrangements

↗ Process

1. State that the purpose of this part of the session is to begin to look at the role of supervision within the workplace.
2. Divide group into threes and fours. Ask them to discuss and make notes on the following questions (which can be written on the board or flipchart):
   - What do you mean by the term 'supervision'?
   - What is the purpose of supervision?
   - Share your experiences of supervision, both positive and negative.
3. After about 20 minutes, return to the large group. Each group should feed back in turn on question 1, then on question 2. Groups should be asked to feed back on question 3 only to the extent that they wish to share. Main points can be noted on flipchart.
4. Distribute handout *The Objectives of Supervision*. Go through the handout, and ensure that all participants are clear about the role of supervision as a means of giving support, for ensuring accountability, and for enabling professional development.
5. Distribute handouts *Supervision Modes* and *Supervision Arrangements*. Encourage discussion about how the information given on the handouts compares with current or previous experience of supervision; and what these handouts may offer in terms of looking more creatively at different options for supervision practice.
6. State that in a future module, there will be the opportunity to plan and implement a supervision system that is appropriate to the specific circumstances operating within this team. In the meantime, there is the opportunity to look at how skills so far developed may be used within a supervision context.

 Exercise 7.6: Developing Supervision Skills

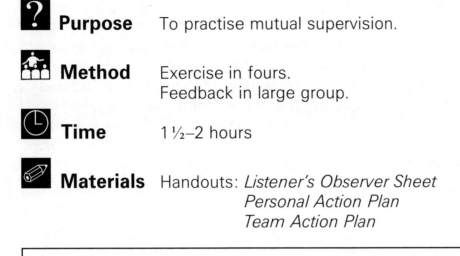

Purpose   To practise mutual supervision.

Method   Exercise in fours.
Feedback in large group.

Time   1½–2 hours

Materials   Handouts: *Listener's Observer Sheet*
Personal Action Plan
Team Action Plan

Note to Group Leader: In the following exercise, team members will be encouraged to give each other positive and critical feedback. It may be helpful to remind them of the guidelines for giving and receiving feedback (see Module 4), and to suggest that they briefly re-read the relevant handouts before the start of this exercise.

Process

1. Ask participants to divide into groups of 3–4, (A, B, C and D), preferably with different people to the previous exercise.
2. Initially A and B are supervisor and supervisee respectively, with C and D being observers. As supervisee, B identifies an issue relevant to the work situation that is causing concern. A should listen, help B to clarify what the difficulties are, and help them explore possible alternative ways of tackling the issue.
3. The aim is to use skills so far used during the programme:
   - active listening
   - being sensitive and responding to the feelings aroused in the other
   - giving positive or critical feedback as appropriate and bearing in mind the guidelines for giving and receiving positive and critical feedback. The interchange should take place for up to fifteen minutes.
4. C and D should sit apart from A and B, and take notes, using headings listed on the handout *Listener's Observer Sheet* as a framework. Additional comments can be added as considered appropriate. C and D can also act as timekeepers.
5. At the end of the time, B should feed back to A as to how helpful that session was, and identify any particular positive and negative points. The observers should then state any points that they noted.
6. Roles should then be changed, with, for example, B as supervisor, C as supervisee, D and A as observers.
7. The process is repeated.
8. By the end of the exercise, everyone should have had the opportunity to be supervisor, supervisee, and observer.

9. End the session by returning briefly to the large group, and asking people to share how they felt about this exercise, and to identify any main learning points.

Note to Group Leader: This is another exercise which may raise sensitive issues that are not dealt with adequately within the small group. You should be on the look out for anyone who does not appear particularly comfortable at this stage. It may be worth repeating the statement that if an issue has arisen for someone that is causing them concern, they should at some stage share it, either with you as group leader, their line manager, or some other person whom they feel might be helpful.

---

10. Action Planning
    - Each person should be encouraged to complete a Personal Action Plan as an outcome of the day's session.
    - The team could agree a Team Action Plan, as a result of awareness and learning gained from the day.
    - Opportunity should be given to review progress on previously agreed Team Action Plans, if these are not being regularly reviewed at other times.

🔲 Handout: Listener's Observer Sheet

Make notes on what you observe in the following areas:

Seating position:

Body posture:

Eye contact:

Facial expressions:

Tone and loudness of voice;

Speed in talking:

Verbal responses:

▣ Handout: Empathic Listening

In the following dialogues, tick the response which you think most clearly reflects empathy, i.e. appears to understand and reflect the other person's feelings.

Example Dialogue

Student

You know, I find it really hard to decide what I want to do. My father wants me to get a job. My mother wants me to go to college. I can't please both of them, and neither of them may be right.

Teacher

(a) Well, it's up to you to make your own decision.
(b) You're confused and finding it difficult to decide what is right for you. Your parents are not agreed about what you should do; and you're wondering whether either of them really provides the best solution.
(c) Let's look at why you would like to please your parents. One of them is bound to be disappointed.

Comments

(a) Patronising statement; advising.
(b) Communicates good understanding.
(c) Interprets the meaning of what is said; makes assumptions.

Dialogue 1. Young person

I'm really fed up with getting into trouble with the police. Me and my mates used to think that nicking things from shops was fun, but now I'm not sure that it's worth it in the long run.

Youth Worker

(a) I am sure your parents would be pleased if you didn't get into more trouble. They have been very worried about you.
(b) I can understand what you are feeling, and am glad you have made the decision to go straight.
(c) You now feel that stealing is giving you more hassle than its worth: taking things from shops is not the same as it used to be.

Dialogue 2. Team Member to Colleague

I know I'm being stupid, but I'm worried about my operation, both whether something will go wrong with it, and whether I will be in pain afterwards.

Colleague

(a) You feel silly that you're worried, but would like to be given some reassurance that it will be all right, and that you will not be in too much pain.

(b) I know I would be worried in your shoes, but you have a good doctor, don't you?

(c) It's quite usual for people to worry, but worrying about it will not really help you that much.

(d) I'm sure you'll be able to cope: it probably won't hurt that much.

Dialogue 3. 15 Year-Old-Girl to Social Worker

I've been to the doctor and she's told me that I'm pregnant. I've really had a shock, because it wasn't planned. My boyfriend and I are quite pleased, but my Dad is going to go mad. He said he would disown me if ever I got pregnant!

Social worker

(a) You're really a bit young to have a baby. It might be a good idea to consider having an abortion.

(b) I can understand you not knowing what to do. You sound as though you need some counselling.

(c) I wouldn't make a decision yet as to what to do. Wait until you've had some time to calm down and think.

(d) You sound as though you're wanting what's best for you and your boyfriend but are fearing your Dad's response.

Dialogue 4. Residential Carer in Home for Older People to Staff Counsellor

I love the job, but my husband is trying to persuade me to leave. He doesn't like me working shifts, and wants me home at week-ends. But he's not in much himself. He goes off playing golf most Saturdays and Sundays.

Staff counsellor

(a) You're feeling pressurised to leave a job which means a lot to you, and think that your husband is being unfair in what he is asking you to do.

(b) I suppose you could ask your husband to compromise: you say you will give up the job if he gives up his golf!

(c) You have to make up your own mind what to do: at the end of the day, it's your life.

(d) Your husband has a point. Residential work can put a lot of pressure on family life, and it would not help you to put your personal happiness at risk.

📄 Handout: The Objectives of Supervision

1. To provide support for team members.
2. To ensure that staff are clear about their roles and responsibilities.
3. To ensure that practice within the team is consistent with organisational policy and procedures.
4. To provide staff with the opportunity to identify areas for professional development, and to enable them to acquire greater awareness, knowledge and skills in these areas.

📄 Handout: Supervision Modes

Formal	Mode
1. Supervision takes the form of planned meetings on an individual or group basis. There is an agreed agenda and methods for reaching objectives. Such meetings can be arranged for a limited or indefinite period of time, and for general or specific purposes. (*For example, a Manager contracts with her deputy to meet with him once a week for an hour to discuss issues relevant to managing the team. Both contribute items to the agenda, which is agreed at the beginning of the session.*)	2. Supervision takes the form of unplanned discussions and consultations on an individual or group basis. The agenda is agreed on the spot; often when an unforeseen crisis or problem has arisen. However, some space and time is created away from service-delivery to work on the problem. (*For example, a young person in a residential home has barricaded herself in her bedroom, and is stating that she is not going to come out until the residential social worker agrees to give her back the snooker cues and balls, which have been confiscated from her. The shift leader sits down with the member of staff to explore how the situation should best be handled.*)
Planned	**Ad Hoc**
3. Agreements are reached between individuals and members of a group to give help, advice, constructive criticism, and other forms of feedback, while working with those for whom they are providing a service. These agreements are made in advance, according to predetermined objectives, and made subject to monitoring and regular review. (*For example, during a staff meeting, a youth worker acknowledges that he does not handle difficult situations with young people well; he tends to become aggressive too quickly, and hence the situation escalates rather than is diffused. Other youth workers agree to observe him at these times, to give him advice when appropriate, and to provide him with feedback as soon after an incident as possible*).	4. Supervision is given while individuals are working with service users, or engaged in service delivery tasks. It may take the form of help, advice, constructive criticism or offered through demonstration and example. This activity may become the focus for discussion in a more formal context, or be developed into an explicit supervision agreement; but first occurs as unplanned activity because of needs and circumstances. (*For example, a new member of staff and an experienced teacher accompany a group of students on an outing to the local botanic gardens. The new member of staff meets one of his friends there, and spends time talking to him. The other teacher interrupts him; on their return, later in the day, she initiates a discussion about responsibilities when supervising children.*)
Informal	**Mode**

Based on Payne C. and Scott T. (1982) *Developing Supervision of Teams in Field and Residential Social Work, Part 1, Papers No. 12*. National Institute for Social Work.

📄 Handout: Supervision Arrangements

Individual supervision		Traditional Model. One-to-one discussion focusing on professional concerns or problems, and the development of the individual worker.
Pairs		Supervisor supervises two workers whose needs are similar. Enables greater range of discussion.
Peer supervision		Two experienced workers supervise each other. Often priority is given to supportive function.
Attachment		A more experienced staff member supervises a less experienced staff. Supervisor retains overall responsibility.
Group		Group of staff with similar needs work together to identify and meet those needs. Often priority is given to supportive function. Supervisor may facilitate process.
Colleague group		Group works together on a specified task. Supervisor monitors process.
Team		Whole team works together, regardless of needs or tasks. Focuses on the work of the team itself, as in team meetings.

Adapted from Payne C. and Scott T. (1982) *Developing Supervision of Teams in Field and Residential Social Work, Part 1, Papers No. 12*. National Institute for Social Work.

📑 Handout: Personal Action Plan

Title of session:

Date:

What I have learned from this session is:

What I have learned is relevant to my practice in the following ways:

As a result of what I have learned, I have identified the following goals for myself:

In order to achieve these goals, I need to:

Factors that might help me achieve my goals are:

Factors that might hinder me from achieving my goals are:

I can increase the helping factors by:

I can lessen the influence of hindering factors by:

Content of action plan discussed with:

Date on which I will review progress of this action plan:

📄 Handout: Team Action Plan

What is our agreed goal?

In order to achieve our goal, what needs to be done? (Make a list of all tasks).

Who is going to be responsible for ensuring that each of the identifed tasks are undertaken (different people can be identified for different tasks).

What factors might help us to achieve our goal?

What factors might hinder us achieving our goal?

How can we increase helping factors?

How can we lessen the influence of hindering factors?

When will we review progress on what has been agreed? (For example, it may be decided to put it on the staff meeting agenda in three months time).

Who is to take responsibility for ensuring that the agreed Action Plan is implemented? (This need not be a person who is actually involved in implementing the Action Plan).

Further Reading

Atherton, J. (1986) *Professional Supervision in Group Care*. Tavistock
    Publications.
d'Ardenne, P.and Mahtaani, A. (1989) *Transcultural Counselling in Action*. Sage
    Publications.
Hawkins, P. and Shohet, R. (1989) *Supervision in the Helping Professions*. Open
    University Press.
Murgatroyd, S. (1985) *Counselling and Helping*. British Psychological Society,
    Methuen.
Nelson-Jones, R. (1983) *Practical Counselling Skills*. Holt, Rinehart and Winston.
Nelson-Jones, R. (1986) *Human Relationship Skills*. Holt, Rinehart and Winston.
Payne, C.and Scott, T. (1982) *Developing Supervision of Teams in Field and
    Residential Social Work, Parts 1 and 2*. National Institute of Social Work.

The Payne and Scott NISW papers are excellent in providing a basis for
consideration of supervision practice, and are the source of handout material
used in this module. Any group leader not experienced in considering different
types of supervision would benefit from acquiring these as reference material.
They could also be used if a team wished to do further detailed work on
supervision practice and structures.

Module 8: Developing Sensitive and Collaborative Forms of Communication

? Aims

To encourage team members to communicate with each other with sensitivity, and to identify collaborative ways of resolving problems.

◎ Objectives

1. To identify the dangers of placing labels on people.
2. To develop open and honest communication between team members.
3. To understand the processes involved when experiencing a major life change.
4. To learn to use a framework for resolving problems in a supportive and collaborative way.

⊡ Structure of Module

1. Exercise 8.1: The Dangers of Labelling
2. Exercise 8.2: Developing Open and Honest Communication
3. Input by Group Leader: Understanding Transition and Change
4. Exercise 8.3: Personal Experience of Transition
5. Exercise 8.4: A Framework for Problem-Solving
6. Further Reading

✎ Materials Required

Flipchart, pens, blu-tack, A4 paper, pens or pencils, sticky labels or pieces of card, sellotape or paper clips.

Copies of handouts:
- *Encouraging Open and Honest Communication between Team Members*
- *Reactions Experienced During a Time of Change*
- *Understanding and Managing Personal Change*
- *A Framework for Problem-Solving*
- *Instructions for Problem-Solving Exercise*
- *Observer Sheet*

✓ Exercise 8.1: The Dangers of 'Labelling'

? Purpose   To experience what it is like to be 'labelled'.

Method   Exercise in large group.

🕐 Time   20–25 minutes.

✏️ Materials   Sticky labels, or alternatively pieces of card about ½" × 2", each with a different role, mood or characteristic written on it, e.g. leader, bossy, the joker, kind, boring, lazy, good-humoured, a hard worker, impatient, depressed, etc.

The aim is for each person to wear the label in such a way that they cannot see their own but can see all others within the group. Thus, the sticky label can be placed by the group leader on the person's forehead; if card is used, it can be worn as a headband, and attached at the back of the head with sellotape or a paper clip, in such a way that the writing is to the front.

Note to Group Leader: This exercise can be used as an ice-breaker at the beginning of the day, and approached as a 'game', rather than taken too seriously. However, there is obviously an underlying serious message, which needs to be pointed out at the end.

↗ Process

1. Input by Group Leader
The following information can be used to provide the basis for the exercise.

❝ We all have perceptions as to how we see other people's qualities and personality characteristics. For example, we may view someone as 'reliable' or a 'time waster'. As a consequence, our behaviour towards that person is often directly influenced by what we think about them. The aim of this exercise is to view the effects of this both on ourselves, and on others involved.

Each person is to wear a label on which is written a quality or personality. The label will be worn in such a way that everyone else in the group can see the writing, but the wearer will not know what it says.

You are being asked to pretend that you have agreed to go on holiday together as a group. However, you have not yet decided what kind of a holiday, where it is to be, where you stay, how long you go for, etc. You have agreed to meet in order to make some decisions about this. This is the meeting. The main point is that during the discussion, you have got to behave to each other according to the labels that people are wearing. ❞

2. Place the labels on people, ensuring that the wearer does not see their own.
   Let the discussion run for five to ten minutes. If necessary, insert a few comments yourself, to ensure that everyone is getting some response to their label.

3. Ask each person in turn what they thought was on their label. If anyone is having difficulties in guessing, additional comments can be made which might help them, e.g. for someone seen as 'reliable', the comment might be, 'If you say you will get the foreign currency, people will feel they can depend on you to do so without having to chase you up about it.'

4. Gain people's comments about their experience of the exercise:
   - How did a specific perception of another person affect your verbal or non-verbal responses?
   - What did it feel like to be on the receiving end?

5. Finish by pointing out that, if we are perceived in a certain way, and people respond to us accordingly, then we are liable in time to acquire those characteristics. For example, if someone sees us as not skilled at cooking, we will either be deprived of the opportunities to acquire those skills, or if we get consistently negative comments about the cooking that we do, we are likely to lose confidence, and become worse rather than better.

   Our attitudes and actions towards our colleagues, and to others we work with, can have a direct effect on how they perceive themselves, and consequently, on how they behave.

✓ Exercise 8.2: Developing Open and Honest Communication

? **Purpose**   To explore the issues involved in developing open and honest communication between team members.

Method   Exercise in pairs.
Feedback in large group.

🕐 **Time**   30–40 minutes (if exercise is repeated, this time is doubled).

Materials   Handouts: *Encouraging Open and Honest Communication between Team Members*.

↗ **Process**

1. Input by group leader

   ❝ Often in our work, we may be expecting service users, and perhaps other team members, to share aspects of their thoughts and feelings that they have reservations about sharing. Many of us have difficulty with this. However, if we are not able to be more open in our communication with each other, how can we expect others to be open with us? This is an exercise that enables you to explore some of the issues around 'open and honest communication'. ❞

2. Give out handout *Encouraging Open and Honest Communication between Team Members*. Ask participants to partner with someone whom they do not work closely with, or know so well, and to follow the instructions as written. Remind the group of previous work done on giving and receiving feedback.

3. After about twenty minutes, return to large group. Lead a discussion which includes the following points and questions:
   • Was that difficult?
   • Why?
   • Why should we be able to do it?
   These are not difficult questions. If we cannot do this with each other, how can we expect others to share intimate information with us? Do we expect service users and other workers to trust us, when we cannot trust and share with each other?

4. Participants sometimes find this exercise so useful, enjoyable, and unexpectedly rewarding, that they wish to repeat it with a different partner. If this were to happen, and everyone were in agreement, people could create their own questions, as long as the basic ground rules continue to apply.

❏ Input by Group Leader: Understanding Transition and Change

❛ Within our work, we will often encounter people who are involved in a process of transition. Obvious times of change include death of a person close to them, break-up of their family, loss of an important relationship, or starting a new school or job. Leaving one life stage and entering another is also in itself a significant transitional event. The greater number of changes that a person experiences either at the same time, or in close proximity to each other, the more pressure and stress will be experienced by that person.

To help someone deal with these changes constructively, it is helpful to be aware of the phases that people go through when they are experiencing change, and to recognise the symptoms of stress that may arise as a result. This may also be useful for staff to know in relation to themselves, as they too will encounter many changes and crises in both their personal and professional lives! ❜

Give out handout *Reactions Experienced During a Time of Change.* Ask team members to read this.

Note to Group Leader: Understanding the effects of change on individuals is crucial for staff who regularly work with people experiencing major changes in their lives. If this is an area that is not familiar to you, it would be worthwhile to read the relevant chapter by Barrie Hopson (details given at end of Handout) before this session.

✓ Exercise 8.3: Personal Experience of Transition

? Purpose To increase understanding of the effects of change on a person's life, and factors that help ease the stress involved.

Method Exercise individually.
Exercise in threes.
Feedback in large group.

🕐 Time 30–40 minutes.

✏ Materials Handout: *Understanding and Managing Personal Change*

↗ Process

1. Give out handout *Understanding and Managing Personal Change*.
2. Ask each person to complete this on their own, giving an example that they would be willing to share within a small group.
3. After about ten minutes, divide the team into groups of 3–4.
4. Within these groups, each person in turn should share what they have written.
5. After about 20–30 minutes, return to large group.
6. Ask for general feedback on what people learned from that exercise. Look specifically for factors that help people cope with change, and factors that make the process of coping with change a difficult one. Key points can be put up on flipchart paper.

Exercise 8.4: A Framework for Problem-Solving

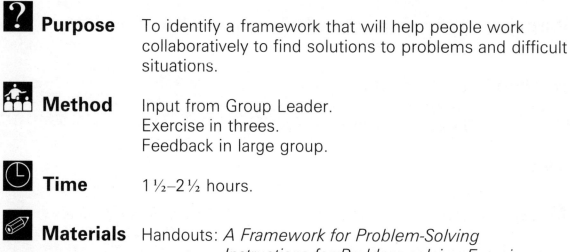

Purpose   To identify a framework that will help people work collaboratively to find solutions to problems and difficult situations.

Method   Input from Group Leader.
Exercise in threes.
Feedback in large group.

Time   1 ½–2 ½ hours.

Materials   Handouts: *A Framework for Problem-Solving*
Instructions for Problem-solving Exercise
Observer Sheet

Process

1. Input by Group Leader

   ❝ Problem-solving is integral to all that we do. In work situations, there are constantly problems to be solved. The team development programme itself may throw up many. If these are to be resolved pro-actively, they invariably require decisions to be made. The more co-operative and open the decision-making process, the more likely long-term sustainable solutions are likely to be identified.

   This process can be helped through having a structure to guide thinking and action. Most problems which people face in day-to-day work come attached to people. Getting the human element right is needed for a successful solution. Unless members of staff teams are good at problem solving, the quality of the service they offer will be adversely affected, and the stress levels of all will be unacceptably increased.

   Successful problem-solving benefits from a systematic approach. This involves a shared understanding from those involved as to how the problem looks from the presenter's point of view. It requires an exploration to find the source of the problem and to identify what has to change. The next stage is the agreement of practical and measurable goals, adequate to bring about change, and a monitoring of their success.

   It is helpful to have a framework that will encourage a collaborative and supportive approach to resolving problems and difficulties, and will enable the most effective outcome to be achieved. ❞

2. Give out handout *A Framework for Problem-Solving*. Point out that the sections that most people gloss over are the analysis of the problem, and the brainstorming of different solutions, but that both of these are essential if the best possible solution to a problem is to be found. For example, the tendency is to get attracted by an early solution, and to start to follow through the next stages as though that has been the one that has been determined. However, a major part of this process is to keep the mind

completely open about ways forward until all possible ideas, both likely and unlikely ones, have been aired and recorded. Only then should the process of evaluation and selection be started.

3. It can be helpful to work an example through with the team to show them how the framework might be used. This can be prepared beforehand, and may be based on an issue that is relevant to the workplace.

4. Distribute handouts *Instructions for Problem-Solving Exercise* and *Observer Sheets*. Ask the group to divide into groups of three. Each person should have a turn to be the presenter of a problem, a supporter or facilitator, and an observer. If there needs to be four in a group, then each person can be an observer twice. About 30 minutes should be allowed for each problem.

5. Suggest that the person presenting the problem selects one that is real for them: this exercise does not work well on fabricated difficulties. Conversely, people have found that unexpected solutions to situations that they have perceived to be intractable have arisen out of this process when undertaken properly. State that what is shared in the small groups should remain confidential to that context. There will be a brief feedback in the large group afterwards, but this will focus on evaluating the usefulness of the framework, rather than asking people to talk about any of the content.

6. When all people have had a chance in each of the roles, bring them back together for a short feedback in the large group. Ask each group in turn to comment on their evaluation of the usefulness of the feedback. People can also be requested to make comments on their experience of the different roles. Observers in particular can be requested to state to what extent the presenter and facilitator were able to keep to the framework, and whether they either deviated from it, or skipped over some of the stages. Reinforce the principle that the real value of this process is to ensure that proper attention is paid to each phase.

7. State that this framework can be usefully used in both staff meetings and supervision as a means of providing a structured and comprehensive approach to approaching difficult situations.

⬛ Handout: Encouraging Open and Honest Communication Between Team Members

This exercise helps team members to be more open with each other. The following ground rules apply:

- Take turns asking questions, choosing them in any order.
- Ask only those questions which you are prepared to answer.
- Any member may decline to answer any question asked of them.
- Subsidiary questions may be asked to ensure that replies are fully understood.
- Participants should agree that answers are to remain confidential.
- Questions may be asked more than once.

Questions to be Asked in any Order

- Are you happy in your present job?
- Are you effective in your present job?
- What do you see as the next step in your career development?
- What personal weaknesses inhibit your performance?
- What do you regard as your major strengths?
- What are your main development needs?
- What are the principal achievements you are looking for in your work right now?
- Where do you see yourself ten years from now?
- What do you think that I think of you?
- What do you think of me?
- Describe your different responsibilities?
- What was your first impression of me when we first met?
- How do you respond to pressure?
- Are you enjoying this activity?
- What barriers do you see to your own advancement?
- What do you see as my greatest strength?
- What do you see as my greatest weakness?
- What do you see as the greatest strength of this staff team?
- What do you see as the greatest weakness of this staff team?
- To whom are you closest in our team? Why do you think that is?
- What is the major contribution you make to our team?
- Do you receive sufficient feedback from other team members?

Close the activity by each person answering the following:

- How could we better help each other in our work?
- How else can we jointly improve the effectiveness of our team?

▣ Handout: Reactions Experienced During a Time of Change

Whatever the nature of change in a person's life, there is a predictable response in terms of feelings and reaction. Very often, individuals may feel that the strong, negative emotions which threaten to overwhelm belong to them alone. It can be helpful to understand that these are common human responses, and if worked through appropriately, will not last for ever, nor prove to be destructive.

The seven stages can be summarised as follows:

1. **Immobilisation**
This is a feeling of being overwhelmed by what is happening. There is an inability to understand or plan for the future. This stage has been described as feeling 'frozen up'. The more negative and unfamiliar this stage appears, the more intensely this stage is experienced.

2. **Minimisation**
At this point, the person attempts to make the implications of the situation appear less than they are—even to the stage of denying that any change exists. To an onlooker, this may appear to be an unhelpful response, with the person refusing to acknowledge reality. However, this may in fact be a necessary phase in the adjustment process, when the immediate situation may prove too traumatic for immediate acknowledgement. Hence, a period of external denial provides opportunity for the subconscious to come to terms with what has happened, and prepare the conscious self for eventual acceptance.

3. **Depression**
When eventually, the conscious self accepts what has happened, severe depression can result. This depression is normally an outcome of feeling out of control, not able to prevent or influence the unwanted changes. There can be periods of changing and intensely experienced emotions which generate considerable energy, including extreme anger, followed by feelings of total apathy and hopelessness.

4. **Letting Go**
Eventually, there comes an acceptance that the new reality has to be faced and accepted. This is the start of psychologically detaching self from the situation that existed prior to the change. Optimism may be expressed about the future.

5. **Testing**
After 'letting go' of the past, the person may start trying out new behaviours and ways of managing the changed situation.

6. **Search for Meaning**
The person may then start to try to understand why the situation had to change, and in what ways they are different. The desire to make sense and give meaning to the changes that occur in their lives is very strong.

7. **Internalisation**

Finally, this newly acquired meaning becomes an internalised part of their behaviour.

In summary the seven phases represent a cycle of experiencing a disruption, acknowledging its reality, trying out new behaviour within the changed situation, trying to reach some understanding of what is happening and why, and finally incorporating changes into one's behaviour.

Throughout this process, the level of morale may vary, as the diagram below shows.

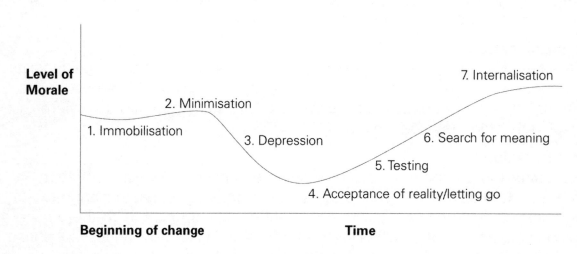

It is important to be aware that individuals do not move in a smooth manner from phase to phase. Often, they may stay longer in one phase than another, or may return to a previous stage. However, it can be helpful to know that these different stages, and the often traumatic emotions that are associated with them, are part of a natural process, and that they can pass.

Each person's experience of this cycle is different, and will be influenced by many factors, including previous experiences of change, levels of support received, and the extent to which the change was expected and predicted.

(Adapted from Hopson, Transition: Understanding and Managing Personal Change. from Herbert, M. *Psychology for Social Workers*, 1986.)

Handout: Understanding and Managing Personal Change

1. Think of a period of time which you experienced as being traumatic.

2. Identify your immediate reaction, and any subsequent feelings you experienced?

3. What steps did you take to cope?

4. Who, if anyone, offered help?

5. Which of these offers did you find helpful, which unhelpful?

📖 Handout: A Framework for Problem-Solving

1. **Define the Problem**
   Identify the issue that is causing concern.

2. **Analyse the Problem**
   Gain as much information concerning the problem as is possible:
   (a) Why is this causing concern?
   - What is happening?
   - When?
   - How often?
   - Who is involved?
   (b) Who else is evaluating the situation as a problem? Why?

3. **Brainstorm Alternative Solutions**
   (a) Suggest a range of alternative solutions, without rejection or evaluation of ideas.
   (b) Suspend judgement of ideas at this point.

4. **Evaluate Alternative Solutions**
   (a) State your opinion in relation to choice of alternatives.
   (b) Listen to other people's viewpoints.
   (c) Consider any decision to be tentative till a final decision is made.

5. **Decide on Best Alternative**
   (a) Ensure all involved have a commitment to carrying out the decision.
   (b) Clarify any barriers to obtaining this commitment (Each of these barriers represent a problem in itself, which needs to form the focus of a problem-solving process!).

6. **Form Action Plan**
   (a) Identify main goal.
   (b) Identify other objectives that need to be achieved in order to reach this main goal.
   (c) Plan for implementation:
   - What must be done?
   - Who should do what, and by when?
   - Are there any other factors that need to be taken into consideration?

7. **Implementation and Evaluation**
   (a) Implement plan.
   (b) Evaluate outcome.
   (c) Redress any issues that are unsatisfactory.
   (d) If necessary, go back to a previous stage.

▣ Handout: Instructions for Problem-Solving Exercise

As presenter: Identify a problem that is real to you.
Present this problem to your 'supporter or facilitator'.

As supporter or facilitator: Listen to the problem presented to you. Using the problem-solving framework to try to work collaboratively with the person presenting the problem. The aim is to develop some understanding of the nature of the problem, establish appropriate jointly agreed goals, and establish how they might be achieved.

As observer: Observe the supporter or facilitator, and give them feedback in relation to their ability to use the problem-solving framework and the level of communication skills used. Comment particularly on the behaviour noted on the Observer Sheet (next).

■ Handout: Observer Sheet

In the situation you are observing, take note of the verbal and non-verbal behaviour that is being used. Comment specifically on the following:

Speech content:

Eye contact:

Posture:

Gestures:

Facial expression:

Timing:

Voice tone, volume, etc.:

Evidence of sensitive response to the issues raised:

Ability to work collaboratively with the person presenting the problem:

Further Reading

Herbert, M. (1986) *Psychology for Social Workers*. Macmillan.

Jewitt, C. (1982) *Helping Children Cope with Separation and Loss*. Batsford Academic.

Carter, R. et al. (1984) *Systems Management and Change*. The Open University.

Module 9: Establishing a Supervision System

❓ Aim

To plan an initial structure for supervision practice within a team.

◎ Objectives

1. To review awareness and knowledge gained in relation to supervision objectives, arrangements and modes.
2. To look at the role of power within supervision practice, and to consider how supervision can be used to empower all staff.
3. To agree a system of supervision that is appropriate to the needs and circumstances of the team.

▱ Structure of Module

1. Exercise 9.1: Supervision Revisited
2. Exercise 9.2: The Role of Power in Supervision
3. Exercise 9.3: Negotiating a Supervision System
4. Exercise 9.4: Agreeing a Supervision Contract
5. Further Reading

> Note: This module only has a relevance if team members and their manager feel there is a value in developing an alternative model to the traditional one-to-one hierarchical system that is often seen to be the norm. There can be many benefits in exploring a different structure, which can include spreading the work-load, and enabling a more diverse and richer experience of supervision.

✎ Materials Required

Flipchart, pens, blu-tack, A4 paper, pens or pencils.

Copies of handouts:
- *Establishing a Supervision Contract*
- *Example of a Supervision System*

Note to Group Leader: Information given in the form of handouts to participants in this module is not extensive. As group leader, your main role lies in facilitating the process by which clear agreement can be reached as to an appropriate supervision system. If time and the energies of the team allows, then more detailed analysis of current practice and possible structures can be undertaken, as clearly laid out in Payne and Scott, (1982). However, in reality this time is often not available. The main principle is that everyone be involved in some way in the process of understanding the alternatives and participating in the decision-making.
In supporting the group, it would be useful for you to have gained a clear awareness of what the needs and circumstances of the team are, so that you are in a position to make positive contributions and suggestions as relevant.

✓ Exercise 9.1: Supervision Revisited

? Purpose   To recall previous work undertaken on supervision.

Method   Discussion in pairs.
                Feedback in large group.

Time   15–20 minutes.

Materials   Paper and pens.

↗ Process

1. State the aim and objectives of the day's session. Remind team members that the idea of supervision was considered earlier, in Module 7.
2. Ask participants to pair up with a person sitting next to them, and to recall what they can about the material on supervision from the earlier module. Handouts can be referred to. If any further work has been done on supervision since that module, this can also be shared.
3. After about ten minutes, participants should return to the group; each pair in turn can feed back briefly what they recalled.
4. Ensure that the following are mentioned from Module 7:
   - The exchange of previous experiences of supervision, both positive and negative.
   - The exploration of the purpose of supervision (giving support, ensuring accountability, enabling professional development).
   - The discussion of different possible modes and arrangement for supervision practice.
   - The opportunity to practise mutual supervision as a means of giving and receiving support.

Exercise 9.2: The Role of Power in Supervision

 **Purpose** To analyse how power might be used and abused within supervision.
To consider how to minimise the possibility of abuse of power.

Method Discussion in small groups.
Feedback in large group.

Time 30–40 minutes (considerably longer if the exercise described in item 4 of Process below is included).

Materials Flipchart paper and pen.

Process

1. Divide team members into small groups for about twenty minutes to consider the following two questions:
   ● In what ways might supervision practice increase inequalities in power?
   ● How might the potential for unequal power relationships arising out of the supervision process be addressed?
2. On returning to the large group, the group leader should note on flipchart paper the main responses arising out of the feedback from both of these questions.
3. During the feedback, the following should be included:
   Issues arising out of Exercise 2.4, *Power and Powerlessness* (in Module 2) should be highlighted. Thus, there are issues for black people having white supervisors, in terms of re-inforcing an already existing imbalance in a power relationship, and similarly, for women being supervised by men.
   The following are a number of ways that can be worked on within a staff team to counteract the potentially oppressive nature of supervision:
   ● A supervision system should take into consideration the factors that might exacerbate a power imbalance, and plan ways of counteracting this. For example, two black members of staff might be involved in peer supervision for the purpose of support, and to explore ways of furthering professional development. If there is only one black member of staff, or a suitable supervision arrangement within the establishment is not feasible, then the possibility of receiving supervision from an appropriate person outside the team should be explored. The superviser should be encouarged to contribute to the selection process to ensure their supervision needs are met.
   Similarly, any individual who by virtue of gender, culture, etc., has specific needs that should be recognised, should have full opportunity to have these acknowledged and addressed in planning a supervision system.
   ● Every supervisory relationship should be based on an agreed contract. (The idea of contracts within supervision is to be covered later in the module). Within this contract, any existing power imbalances should be

identified, acknowledged, with the feelings of all shared, and methods for addressing these imbalances discussed.

- The ability to be assertive is crucial, so that people are able to challenge an inappropriate situation, that team members are able to share what they feel in an open and honest way, and to give constructive critical feedback without feeling that this will have a negative 'rebound' effect on them, is essential.
- Increased sensitivity towards individuals who do feel disempowered and oppressed is also crucial. Exploring ways in which the principle of 'equality' can be integrated into teamworking, whilst acknowledging different roles and responsibilities which lead to differences in perceived status, needs to be an issue that is explicitly addressed.

4. If members of the team appear to be insufficiently sensitive to the feelings of others within the group, and cannot see why they might feel 'disempowered', it can be useful to include the following exercise:
   (a) Suggest that each person recalls a time when they felt powerless, which they would be willing to share with members of the group. This can be a recent experience, or one that occurred a long time ago. So, for example, it might be an incident that happened as a child, when an adult forced them to do something, or more recently, as a residential worker in a case conference, when an 'expert' totally dismissed what they were trying to say about a person within their care.
   (b) Each person should identify what they felt at the time, and why.
   (c) Ask each person in turn to describe the situation, what they felt, and why.
   (d) Make the point that people's feelings are valid and should be accepted as such, whether or not others either understand or agree with them. A person's reality belongs to them, and should not be dismissed. If people perceive that their feelings are minimised, put down or rejected, then that has an impact on their own feelings of value and self worth.
   (e) Consequently, people's feelings in relation to supervision needs should be sensitively listened to, and given an appropriate response.

Note to Group Leader: This exercise can be a powerful one, because of the strength of feelings that are expressed – feelings of anger, frustration, helplessness and humiliation are frequently communicated. Again, it needs to be facilitated with considerable sensitivity, with attention being paid to points made in the Introduction, Guidance for Group Leaders.

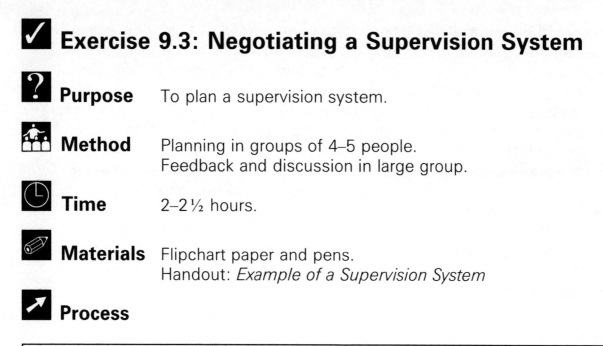

✓ Exercise 9.3: Negotiating a Supervision System

? Purpose   To plan a supervision system.

Method   Planning in groups of 4–5 people.
Feedback and discussion in large group.

Time   2–2 ½ hours.

Materials   Flipchart paper and pens.
Handout: *Example of a Supervision System*

↗ Process

Note to Group Leader: Throughout most of this team programme, managers within the team will probably have been involved in exercises on an equal basis to other members. However, in the following exercise, it may be beneficial to enable the rest of the team to put forward their ideas without managers being present. Often, the need to build in support mechanisms for themselves, or to discuss ways in which they can identify issues that can later be taken up with managers is something that most non-managerial team members prefer initially to share amongst themselves: a form of 'empowerment'! It can be suggested that managers draw up their own proposals, to be given equal status to the others put forward.

1. Remind team members to refer to handouts already given out in Module 7: i.e. *The Objectives of Supervision, Supervision Modes*, and *Supervision Arrangements*. Using these, and bearing in mind points raised during the previous exercise, each group should draw up a suggested supervision structure.
2. Divide into small groups.
3. The group leader should ensure on a regular basis that groups feel they are making constructive progress. They should be made aware that the group leader is available to contribute to the process if they are experiencing difficulties.
4. After 1 ½–2 hours, return to the large group. Alternative proposals should be presented in turn.
5. Strengths and weaknesses of each should be identified, with input from the group leader when appropriate.
6. An effective way of moving forward is to decide as a team which of the suggestions seems to offer the most potential in terms of providing a framework; and then if possible, to incorporate modifications from the other schemes.

7. It should be emphasised that any structure agreed at this point in time will only be provisional in the meantime, and will form the basis of a 'trial run'. It can then be evaluated and modified in the light of experience.
8. The following points should also be made:
   - Establishing a supervision system is not easy. 'Hiccups' are an inevitable part of the process. If it is to work, there needs to be a determination to see it through, as there will be phases when people feel that it does not seem worthwhile. This should be seen as an inevitable part of the process, but should not be allowed to stop progress.
   - The ability to apply this determination depends on keeping in mind the fact that there is a clear purpose to supervision: that ultimately it contributes towards providing a better service. A date needs to be set for a review of the suggested system, when the structure can be changed or updated.

Note to Group Leader: At this point, the proposed system will be in draft form on flipchart paper. It is essential that someone, preferably yourself, takes this, and writes it up in a structured way, incorporating the decisions that have been made. Copies should be distributed to all team members as soon as possible, including a time scale outlining when different sessions will start. A copy of a suggested system arising from one programme is included in the Handout at the end of this module, *Example of a Supervision System*. This example outlines an initial structure for supervision, agreed by members of a staff team. This process took place in a residential setting. Obviously, the professional context in which the team is located will influence the nature of the issues that need to be taken into consideration. The team in this example considered all forms of supervision outlined in the team handout, *Establishing a Supervision Contract* and as a result of extensive discussion, agreed the Example.

Exercise 9.4: Agreeing a Supervision Contract

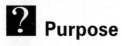 **Purpose**   To establish the purpose of a supervision contract, and to have practice in drawing one up.

Method   Negotiation in pairs or groups.

Time   45+ minutes.

Materials   Handout: *Establishing a Supervision Contract*

Process

1. Input from Group Leader:
   As a means of ensuring that everyone's needs are acknowledged and met within a supervision context, it is important to reach a clear agreement as to expectations, structures, and means of giving each other feedback. Negotiating a clear contract which can be reviewed on a regular basis is an effective means of achieving this end.
2. Give out handout *Establishing a Supervision Contract*, and go through each section with the group. Suggest that this can be used as a framework to help reach a working agreement.
3. Looking at the proposed system of supervision, each person should identify a person or group with whom they will be involved in supervision. Using the handout as a basis for discussion, they should have an initial supervision session, the purpose of which is to draw up a supervision contract that is acceptable to all.

▣ Handout: Establishing a Supervision Contract

A written supervision contract should be negotiated between supervisor and supervisees. This should include agreement in relation to the following areas:

1. Purpose of supervision.
2. How agenda is determined.
3. Decisions about recording: e.g. methods of recording, what is recorded, who records, and where records are kept.
4. Extent to which content of sessions is confidential.
5. Means of evaluating, and giving feedback on supervision experience.
6. Basic ground rules, including, for example:
   - How often sessions take place.
   - How long each session will be.
   - Where sessions are held.
   - Acceptable reasons for cancellation.
   - How cancellations are dealt with.
   - Nature of consultation that takes place between formal sessions.

📃 Handout: Example of a Supervision System

Group Supervision

All were agreed that group supervision could be a valuable form of supervision to introduce into the team.

The aim of group supervision would be to 'improve working practices through mutual support'.

It was decided that there was value in having sessions that were held without managers, and sessions that included managers.

There were predominantly two 'teams' who worked on alternate weekends. It was realised that there was a danger that different working practices could be developed on alternate weekends, and hence there was a need to ensure that there was good communication between the two groups. One way of enabling this was to create two groups for supervision, each group comprising staff covering each weekend.

However, it was also felt that there was value in the staff team covering each weekend to meet together as a group, in order that issues affecting the weekend's working could be addressed. Unless this forum was specifically created, there was no opportunity for staff to do this.

There was value in staff meeting together to discuss issues without managers being present. This gave people the opportunity to raise and explore issues with peers, when perhaps they did not feel sufficiently ready or confident to raise them with the wider staff group. The aim would be to gain other people's perspective on those issues, and to consider whether they warranted being taken up in a different setting. It would be possible to look at the most appropriate forum for raising the issues, and to perhaps identify and practise any skills required in articulating them.

There was also value for these groups to meet with a manager, and to gain an additional perspective on issues under consideration. This forum could then be used to determine whether there was value in putting these items on the agenda of a full staff meeting.

The value of this process was seen to be as follows:

1. All staff would have the opportunity to share what they felt in a 'safe' setting, and hence be provided with a support mechanism that could help them manage their personal stress levels.
2. All staff would gain the opportunity to look at effective ways of raising these issues in a wider forum if considered appropriate.
3. More efficient use could be made of staff meeting time, where many items on the agenda would already have been worked through to a great extent, and may have been distilled to its essential elements. This would prevent meetings being used for the purpose of 'off-loading', as this would have been done in the other forums. Also, some subjects could be fully dealt with in group supervision.

As a result of the different perceived needs, the following 'rolling programme' was devised:

Week 1

12.00–1.00 p.m. Managers Meeting: Team manager and Deputy Team manager.

12.00–1.00 p.m. Group supervision, without managers present.

Group 1: Half staff group.
Group 2: Half staff group.

 Each group would draw up a written agreement or contract, based on the handout *Establishing a Supervision Contract*. The content of this contract should be reviewed on a regular basis, and modified if necessary.

 In an initial discussion of this document, the following 'ground rules' were proposed as providing the basis of an agreement:

1. Supervision sessions should take place in a room with minimal interruptions: e.g. phones off the hook.
2. A session should take place, even if only two people could be present.
3. Everyone within the group should be given the opportunity to contribute towards the agenda, and be given a specific portion of time to enable their issue to be discussed.
4. Managers can ask for an issue to be placed on the group agenda for discussion. The group retain the right to decide whether they feel the group supervision time is an appropriate forum to discuss this issue.
5. Similarly, a member of one group can ask for an issue to be placed on the other group's agenda; again, the second group has the right to determine whether in fact this is an appropriate matter for discussion.
6. Group supervision time should not be used for being critical of individuals not involved in the session. If this should happen, other members of the group have the responsibility to point out that this matter should be raised directly with the person concerned.
7. Minutes of sessions should be taken, and kept in a file; the location of this file would be established within the written agreement or contract drawn up by the group.
8. Limits of confidentiality should be laid down within the written agreement or contract. However, unless there is explicit agreement within the group, all individuals should be able to discuss all topics within one-to-one supervision with their managers, if they wished.

Purpose of session:

1. To provide a forum for any member to discuss issues and share concerns they hold, and to receive support from the group in exploring and discussing these.
2. To look at issues placed on the agenda by individuals outside the group, and to discuss these if it is considered to be appropriate.
3. To agree items to be placed on the agenda for the following week, to be discussed with the Manager.

Week 2

12.00–1.00 p.m.   Group supervision. Membership of group same as in Week 1, but including Team manager or Deputy Team manager.

The two groups should remain the same as the previous week. However, the managers would alternate between groups. Thus, each group would get the opportunity to work with both managers.

Purpose of session:

1. To discuss items placed on the agenda as an outcome of the previous group session.
2. To provide a forum for any member to discuss issues or share concerns they hold, and to receive support from the group in exploring and discussing these.
3. To look at issues placed on the agenda by individuals outside the group, and to discuss these if it is considered to be appropriate.
4. To agree items to be placed on the agenda for the next staff meeting, identifying who is going to be responsible for introducing each issue.

Whereas the previous week may include considerable 'offloading', the aim of this week was to begin to be more focused, and to determine what actions and decisions could or should be made.

Week 3

12.00–1.00 p.m.   Group supervision. Membership of group to be made up of those who had just completed a working weekend.

Purpose of session:

1. To identify and discuss any issues arising from working the previous weekend.
2. To look at ways of improving practice during weekend working.

Weeks 4–6

A repeat of weeks 1–3.

Week 7

A staff training day.

Individual Supervision

Team manager: Deputy plus five members of staff.
Deputy team manager: Five members of staff.
Frequency of supervision: Once every seven weeks.
Acceptable reasons for
postponement:

- Illness of staff member
- Unavoidable rota change
- External meetings
- No other member of staff on duty
- Child's illness requiring special attention.

If a session has to be postponed, an alternative time should be re-arranged as soon as possible.

Induction

One identified person is to take responsibility for co-ordinating the induction process. This person to be formally involved in the role for a period of three months, with a complementary supervisory role to be played by the line manager.

Peer Supervision

Two female members of staff on a similar grade. Frequency and time to be negotiated between themselves.

Implementation Plan

Although the rolling programme covers a seven week time span, there would be factors that would prevent this running smoothly without a break. Holidays, for example, would result in meetings being cancelled or postponed. Hence, a timetable would be drawn up every seven weeks, which would account for any foreseeable events or breaks, and would allow for any necessary modifications.

Further Reading

Atherton, J. (1986) *Professional Supervision in Group Care*. Tavistock Publications.

Hawkins, P. and Shohet, R. (1989) *Supervision in the Helping Professions*. Open University Press.

Payne, C. and Scott, T. (1982) *Developing Supervision of Teams in Field and Residential Social Work, Parts 1 & 2*. National Institute of Social Work.

Module 10: Review and Action Plan

? Aim

To review the extent to which participants feel they have developed the awareness, knowledge, and skills to work effectively as a team; and to agree an action plan for future development.

◎ Objectives

1. To assess areas of strength and weakness within the team.
2. To establish parts of the team development programme which need repeating or re-inforcing.
3. To look at a process of self-evaluation as a means of encouraging reflective practice.
4. To draw up an Action Plan, both for the team and for individuals.

⊞ Structure of Modules

1. Input by Group Leader: Reviewing the Programme
2. Exercise 10.1: Review Questionnaire
3. Exercise 10.2: Creating Your Own Self-Evaluation Guide
4. Exercise 10.3: Developing an Action Plan

Materials Required

Flipchart, pens, blu-tack, A4 paper, pens and pencils.

Copies of handouts:
- *Review Questionnaire*
- *Review Summary*
- *Self-Evaluation Guide*
- *Action Plan*
- *Team Action Plan*
- *Personal Action Plan*

Note to Group Leader: This module should be used in a flexible way. The principle is that participants be given the opportunity to review and evaluate progress, identify priority areas for future development, and agree an action plan. The following exercises provide a number of ways of achieving this. As Group Leader, you should select those which you feel are most appropriate to the current stage of development of the staff team.

🍎 Input by Group Leader: Reviewing the Programme

❝ Formally, this is the final module of the *Team Development Programme*. However, the process of development should not cease, either on a team or individual level. The purpose of today's session is to review what progress has been made, identify any major areas of weakness, and agree a way forward. ❞

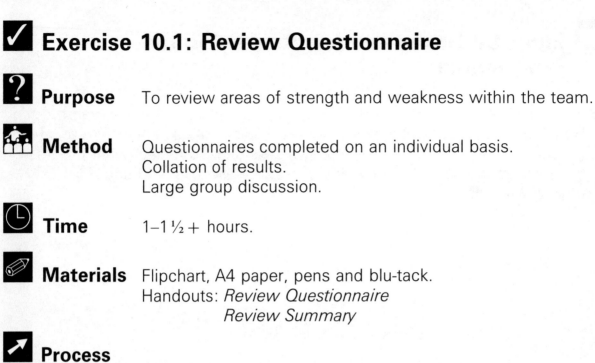

✓ Exercise 10.1: Review Questionnaire

? Purpose   To review areas of strength and weakness within the team.

Method   Questionnaires completed on an individual basis.
Collation of results.
Large group discussion.

🕐 Time   1–1½ + hours.

✎ Materials   Flipchart, A4 paper, pens and blu-tack.
Handouts: *Review Questionnaire*
Review Summary

↗ Process

1. Distribute handouts *Review Questionnaire* and *Review Summary*. State that the questions in this questionnaire are derived from the Aims and Objectives of each of the modules that have been undertaken. Request that people be as honest as possible in their responses.
2. Encourage people to find a space where they are undisturbed by others in the group. Give them sufficient time to complete the questionnaire and summary (about 15 minutes).
3. When everyone has finished, return to the large group.
4. Ask participants to feed back their responses to the last four questions on the summary. As people state them, they should be written up on the flipchart. Repeated responses should be marked with a tick.
5. When everyone has responded, there should be a visual indication of the team perspective. This can be recorded by completing a team response to the last four questions of the summary: i.e. if 'meetings held in the team are generally useful and productive' has received more ticks than any other issue as a perceived 'strength' within the team, then this would be placed first in the collated team response.
6. 'Major strengths' and 'areas where there has been most progress' may not necessarily be the same. For example, team members may always have been very good at 'implementing and adhering to decisions that are made', see that as a major strength, but not have seen much change in that area over the past 12 months; whereas they may feel considerable progress has been made in relation to 'developing the necessary confidence and skills to recognise and challenge oppressive practice', even though it is not yet perceived to be a major strength.
7. Discussion should now be held as to what the implications of the responses are for future action. Has the content of the team development programme been adequately covered? Is there a need to go back over some modules, or part of a module? Are there alternative ways that the issues raised can be addressed?

Exercise 10.2: Creating your own Self-Evaluation Guide

? Purpose To introduce a means of continuing to develop reflective practice within the team through creating a Self-Evaluation Guide.

Method Individual exercise.
Large group discussion.

Time 2+ hours

Materials Handout: *Self-Evaluation Guide*

Process

1. Formal Input by Group Leader:
   Developing a Self-Evaluation Guide presents a means for people to evaluate current practice, and to identify areas which require attention.
2. Distribute handout *Self-Evaluation Guide*.
3. In order to experience how to use the *Guide*, ask people to make a response to those sections that are relevant to what they do.
4. Using the *Guide* as a model, the staff team should then identify areas of practice that they feel are significant in their work.
5. For each area, they can prioritise up to five significant aspects of that area of practice.
6. For each of the five areas, three alternative statements should be made, indicating respectively:
   - Maximum, or most acceptable achievements.
   - In-between achievements.
   - Minimum, and most unacceptable achievements.

7. These statements can then be transferred to a grid.

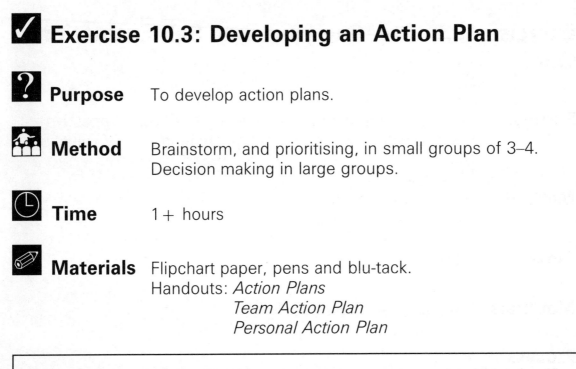

✓ Exercise 10.3: Developing an Action Plan

? Purpose   To develop action plans.

Method   Brainstorm, and prioritising, in small groups of 3–4.
Decision making in large groups.

🕐 Time   1 + hours

Materials   Flipchart paper, pens and blu-tack.
Handouts: *Action Plans*
Team Action Plan
Personal Action Plan

Note to Group Leader: By this stage, team members should be familiar with Action Planning. The following stages replicate almost identically the process outlined in Module 4. However, team members should have considerably more material to use as the basis of planning. In addition, future planning may include addressing issues like:

- Identifying and meeting the training needs of individuals within the team.
- Integrating NVQ assessment into the team.
- Developing specific skill areas: e.g. counselling, working with people who have been sexually abused.
- Establishing team aims and objectives, if these have not been developed or revised since creating a 'Statement of Purpose and Principles'.

Alternative frameworks for Action Plans have been provided, to offer flexibility in how planning is structured. A Personal Action Plan is included; although this module focuses on team action planning, it may be felt important to include some space for individuals to reflect on their own way forward.

↗ Process

1. State the purpose of the exercise.
2. Ask people to divide into small groups. In their groups, they are to review the issues identified from the earlier exercises undertaken.
3. Each group should identify a 'scribe'. For the first few minutes, group members should allow time for brainstorming what issues they feel are significant for the team.
4. After the brainstorming is completed, the group should discuss what has been written; they should then prioritise up to four issues which they wish to see addressed. These should be written on a separate sheet of flipchart paper, which can be put on the wall, or in some place where all can see them.

5. Return to the large group. Each alternative should be considered, with possible ways forward being discussed.
6. Each individual should then decide which four of the suggestions are most valid, and should take priority in being implemented. When everyone has noted their own choice, the group leader should go round the group, asking each person to identify what their choices are, and placing a tick beside the relevant suggestions on the flipchart paper.
7. When everyone's vote has been recorded, the suggestion that has the greatest number of ticks beside it is the first agreed 'goal' which the group should aim to achieve.
8. An Action Plan should then be drawn up, using the handouts *Action Plan* or *Team Action Plan* as a framework for discussion and decision making.

📖 Handout: Review Questionnaire

This questionnaire provides the opportunity to reflect on existing strengths and weaknesses within the team. The questions derive directly from the objectives identified in the ten modules of this book. It will help you reflect on current practice, and should form the basis of your contribution to a team discussion.

Question	Yes/No/Comments
Does the team have a clearly stated and written down Statement of Purpose?	
Does the team have a clearly stated and written down Statement of Principles?	
Does the team have a clearly stated and written down set of Aims and Objectives?	
Was the staff team fully involved in the process of drawing up and agreeing the Statement of Purpose and Principles?	
Do you think that the Statement of Purpose and Principles needs to be reviewed or revised?	
Was the staff team fully involved in the process of drawing up and agreeing the team's Aims and Objectives?	
Do you think that the team's Aims and Objectives need to be reviewed or revised?	
Do you understand what is meant by the term 'stress'?	
Do you think that you recognise and acknowledge the symptoms of stress both in yourself and in others?	
Do you understand what causes stress: i.e. what are the sources of stress?	
Do you know what is meant by 'oppressive practices'?	

Do you feel you have sufficient awareness of the nature of the links between oppressive practices and the experience of stress?	
Is the staff team as a whole sufficiently aware of what oppressive practices take place in the team?	
Have you developed effective ways for managing stress both in your personal and professional life?	
Over the past 12 months, have you become better able to recognise stress, and to manage it more effectively?	
Do you understand what is meant by the term 'assertiveness'?	
Are you aware of the difference between assertive behaviour, and aggressive, manipulative and passive or submissive behaviour?	
Can you identify situations where assertive behaviour is appropriate?	
Do you understand why issues such as race, gender and age affect assertive communication?	
Do team members have the necessary confidence and skills to recognise and challenge oppressive practice?	
Is there evidence that staff negotiate well with each other and with the young people?	
Are difficult situations handled constructively?	
In the last 12 months, do you feel you have become more assertive?	
Do you feel able to give critical feedback in an assertive way?	
Do you feel able to receive critical feedback in an assertive way?	

Do you feel able to give positive feedback in an assertive way?	
Do you feel able to receive positive feedback in an assertive way?	
Are members of the staff team able to appropriately give and receive critical and positive feedback?	
Do you have a clear understanding of the terms 'values' and 'principles'?	
Have you had the opportunity to discuss both your own values, and those held by members of the team?	
Do you have an understanding of how and from where you acquired your own value base?	
Have all members of the staff team been able to constructively discuss the values held by each person as an individual, and the implications of these for practice?	
Has the staff team developed a common professional value base: i.e. established a set of values and principles that underpin your professional practice?	
Do you regularly discuss the implications of translating values and principles into practice with other members of the staff team?	
Is there an agreed way of reaching decisions over issues about which there are strong differences of opinion?	
Are decisions implemented and adhered to?	
Are service users directly involved in the processes of decision-making within the team?	
Do you find that meetings held in the team are generally useful and productive?	

Is everyone's point of view heard?	
Do you feel that you receive sufficient emotional understanding and support from others within the team?	
Are feelings recognised, acknowledged and validated?	
Do staff give each other and the service users the space to share feelings in a supportive and constructive atmosphere?	
Do you receive regular, planned supervision? Does your supervisor have good supervision skills?	
If you are a supervisor, do you feel sufficiently skilled to carry out this role?	
Has the team developed a system of supervision that is appropriate to the needs and circumstances of the team?	
In developing a system of supervision, has imaginative use been made of alternative supervision modes and arrangements?	
Are team members aware of how supervision can potentially involve an abuse of power?	
Have efforts been made to ensure that all staff are empowered, rather than oppressed, through supervision?	
Do you feel that you can trust members of the staff team, and communicate openly and honestly with them?	
Do you feel that there is generally a high level of trust, and open and honest communication, between all members of the staff team?	
In the past 12 months, have team members become more sensitive to the needs of service users in the team?	

Do team members respond to service users as individuals in their own right, and avoid labelling and stereotyping?	
Do you have a good idea of the stages people pass through when experiencing a major life change?	
Do you make considerable efforts to find out what life is like from the perspective of the people in your care?	

🖹 Handout: Review Summary

In the light of this Questionnaire, identify what you perceive to be:

1. Five major strengths within the staff team:

2. Five major weaknesses within the staff team:

3. Areas where you feel most progress has been made over the last 12 months:

4. Areas where you feel least progress has been made over the last 12 months:

5. Any other comments?

▣ Handout: Self-Evaluation Guide

1. Environment	Yes	No	Comments
Monotonous, uniform or harsh colour schemes.			
Some variations, but not well thought out.			
Relaxing and aesthetic use of colour.			
Furniture and fittings are old and in bad condition.			
Furniture and fittings in satisfactory condition, but little variety.			
Furniture and fittings in good condition and varied.			
The basic minimum of furniture and fittings are provided.			
A few pictures are hanging, but little else.			
All rooms have items that add warmth and character, e.g. plants, ornaments.			
No space outside.			
Substantial space outside, but concrete, or otherwise unattractive.			
Pleasant area outside to walk and sit in when weather allows.			

2. Participation	Yes	No	Comments
No involvement by service users in process of writing reports.			
Service users informed as to content of report.			
Service users involved throughout writing of report; encouraged to add own comments.			
Service users never attend case conferences or reviews.			
Service users are allowed to attend part of conferences or reviews.			
Service users encouraged to attend throughout conferences or reviews.			
No formal involvement by service users in decision making about developing the service.			
Staff occasionally discuss issues relevant to developing the service.			
Involvement by service users in decision-making about the service.			
Service has no complaints procedures.			
Complaints procedures, but difficult to understand.			
Complaints procedures accessible to all service users.			

3. Dealing with Conflict	Yes	No	Comments
Staff are often openly hostile to each other.			
Staff often have unresolved conflicts: but not in front of service users.			
Staff get on well: they work out conflicts calmly and constructively.			
Incidents involving violence between staff and service users are common.			
There are often confrontations, but not usually involving violence.			
There is a peaceful atmosphere: very little aggression occurs.			
Aggressive situations are not discussed afterwards.			
Aggressive situations may be talked about informally amongst staff.			
Aggressive situations discussed in supportive way within supervision.			
Recording of aggressive situation is rather ad hoc.			
Formal recording system which briefly outlines actual incident.			
Comprehensive recording system; covers events before, during and after.			

4. Staff Training	Yes	No	Comments
New staff generally thrown in at the deep end.			
Attempt at formal induction, but hit and miss.			
Well worked out induction for all new staff.			
Supervision: what's that?			
Supervision is only ever 'ad hoc'.			
Regular supervision is offered to all staff.			
Staff learn their job mainly 'sitting by Nellie'.			
Occasional training sessions are offered.			
Training covers all key aspects of work.			
'I wouldn't know who to ask for help.'			
Advice and guidance available, on request.			
Guidance and appraisal built into supervision.			
'We don't have staff meetings here.'			
'We call a staff meeting if we need one.'			
Staff meetings are held regularly.			

5. Staff Teamwork	Yes	No	Comments
Staff here work only as individuals.			
Individual staff work well only with 'mates'.			
All staff work well with one another.			
Staff leadership is one of 'divide and rule'.			
Leadership still leaves room for improvements.			
Leadership is firm but fair.			
Staff cover for colleagues only in emergency.			
Staff will cover, but only on special occasions.			
Staff generally willing to cover for colleagues.			
Staff turnover and absenteeism exceeds 25%.			
Staff often absent without adequate explanation or cause.			
Staff on whole absent only when genuinely indisposed.			
Staff meetings are poorly attended.			
Some individuals frequently miss staff meetings.			
Staff meetings are well attended generally.			

6. Communication	Yes	No	Comments
'We don't put much down in writing here'.			
Some recording on daily events, but not much more.			
Records are generally detailed/ comprehensive.			
'Critical incidents' are not always recorded.			
'Critical incidents' are recorded, but not often fully discussed.			
'Critical incidents' are always fully recorded and discussed.			
'Staff meetings: what's the point?'			
'Staff meetings are OK, but sometimes boring.'			
'Staff meetings are really lively.'			
'No one ever really knows what's going on.'			
'I learn most things by talking to my mates.'			
'If I need information, I know who to go to.'			

Handout: Action Plan

After careful examination of all information gained in the preceding sections, complete the following:

A. What areas or issues need to be addressed (indicate order of priority)

B. For each of these areas, suggest specific objectives, targets and outcomes that are required.

C. For each objective, target or outcome to be achieved, identify what needs to be done:

Issues to be Addressed	Objectives	Identified Action

D. Identify factors that might help the achievement of objectives:

E. Identify factors that might hinder the achievement of objectives:

F. How might helping factors be increased?

G. How might the influence of hindering factors be lessened?

H. **Timescales**

In light of the answers above specify actions to be taken:

  (a) By end of first month:

  (b) By end of three months:

  (c) By end of six months:

  (d) By end of 12 months:

I. Establish the date when the **initial** review of the above Action Plan is to be carried out and modified as necessary:

▣ Handout: Team Action Plan

What is our agreed goal?

In order to achieve our goal, what needs to be done? (Make a list of all tasks.)

Who is going to be responsible for ensuring that each of the identified tasks are undertaken (different people can be identified for different tasks.)

What factors might help us to achieve our goal?

What factors might hinder us from achieving our goal?

How can we increase helping factors?

How can we lessen the influence of hindering factors?

When will we review progress on what has been agreed? (For example, it may be decided to put it on the staff meeting agenda in three months time).

Who is to take responsibility for ensuring that the agreed action plan is implemented? (This need not be a person who is actually involved in implementing the action plan.)

▣ **Handout: Personal Action Plan**

Title of session:

Date:

What I have learned from this session is:

What I have learned is relevant to my practice in the following ways:

As a result of what I have learned, I have identified the following goals for myself:

In order to achieve these goals, I need to:

Factors that might help me achieve my goals are:

Factors that might hinder me from achieving my goals are:

I can increase the helping factors by:

I can lessen the influence of hindering factors by:

Content of action plan discussed with:

Date on which I will review progress of this action plan: